Threadplay

with **Libby** **ehman**

*To Virginia,
Enjoy!*
*Libby Lehman
10/00*

Mastering
Machine
Embroidery
Techniques

Brewer
Quilting & Sewing Supplies

DEDICATION

To all threadplayers, past, present, and future. Let the games begin!

ACKNOWLEDGMENTS

I would like to thank the companies who helped with information and products, especially Bernina of America, Inc., Fairfield Processing Corporation, Springs Industries, and Sulky of America.

Thanks to all my families:

That Patchwork Place, which made this project as painless as possible. Thanks in particular to Ursula Reikes for her efficiency and her unerring eye for detail.

The owners of my quilts, who graciously lent them for inclusion in this book.

Mom, Dad, Cathy, Sarah, and Ellen (an animal lover who patiently proofread my writings and defended the feed dogs).

My son, Les, who has enriched my life and quilts by sharing himself and his great fly-tying supplies.

My husband, Lester, whom I thank for both holding me and letting me go. Your love, support, humor, and cooking will always nourish me.

Thanks most of all to my quilting family of fellow teachers, shop owners, and students. You have given me more than I can ever repay.

CREDITS

Editor-in-Chief . . . . Kerry I. Smith
Technical Editor . . . . Ursula Reikes
Managing Editor . . . . Judy Petry
Copy Editor . . . . Tina Cook
Proofreader . . . . Leslie Phillips
Design Director . . . . Cheryl Stevenson
Text Designer . . . . Kay Green
Cover Designer . . . . David Chrisman
Production Assistant . . . . . Marijane E. Figg
Illustrator . . . . Laurel Strand
Photographer . . . . Brent Kane

No part of this product may be reproduced in any form, unless otherwise stated, in which case reproduction is limited to the use of the purchaser. The written instructions, photographs, designs, projects, and patterns are intended for the personal, noncommercial use of the retail purchaser and are under federal copyright laws; they are not to be reproduced by any electronic, mechanical, or other means, including informational storage or retrieval systems, for commercial use.

The information in this book is presented in good faith, but no warranty is given nor results guaranteed. Since Brewer Quilting & Sewing Supplies, Inc. has no control over choice of materials or procedures, the company assumes no responsibility for the use of this information.

This edition first published in 2008
By Brewer Quilting & Sewing Supplies, Inc.
3702 Prairie Lake Ct.
Aurora, IL 60504
Phone: 800-676-6543

ISBN 13: 978-1-889682-49-5

First published in 1997 by That Patchwork Place®, an imprint of Martingale & Company.

Quilt on cover: *Rapture* by Libby Lehman.
Collection of Fairfield Processing Corporation.

Quilt on title page: *Joy Ride* (detail) by Libby Lehman.

Contents

Hidden Agendas (detail)

Preface

$\mathcal{T}$his is all my mother's fault. I do not come from a long line of stitchers, much less quilters. Neither of my grandmothers cared a lick about sewing. Mom did utilitarian sewing and some clothing but did not force it on her four uninterested daughters. Like a lot of my generation, I learned how to use a sewing machine in junior-high homemaking class. I made a charming ensemble out of orange polyester. I then proceeded to make clothing for my sisters and myself. I wasn't particularly good, but I was fast!

In 1971 my mom signed us up for basic quilting lessons. I was very pregnant at the time and would have agreed to anything that offered a distraction. I made an absolutely awful block in chartreuse, orange, and purple, but there was something about the process that intrigued me. For the next ten years I was happy making traditional quilts as a hobby. When Mom opened a shop with two partners (the Quilt Patch in Houston), I began to teach for them. After taking classes with Michael James, Nancy Crow, and Nancy Halpern, my focus shifted from traditional quilts to contemporary art quilts. I now spend almost all my time on quilt-related activities—teaching, lecturing, judging, writing, and most fun of all, making studio art quilts. And to think it all started with my mother trying to distract me. Thanks, Mom—maybe you do know best!

Rapture (detail)

Introduction

This book is the answer to my students who constantly ask, "When are you going to put this all down on paper?" I have been thinking about writing it for awhile, but three things stopped me. One, I was having too much fun making quilts and experimenting with different techniques. Two, I had to work out all the kinks in each technique. Three, and most importantly, I wanted to wait until I had enough new information to make the book a worthwhile investment. I hope you more than get your money's worth.

This is the book I wish I'd had when I began to play with thread. Use it as a reference. "The Basics" on pages 6–29 deals with supplies and information you need to get started. Please read this section before you begin to stitch. "Threadplay Techniques" on pages 30–72 covers methods that can be used independently. If you want to try bobbin drawing, for example, you can go directly to that section and begin.

Most of all, this book is meant to be used. Every sewing machine is different, and there is ample space on these pages for notes so you can record what works best for specific needs. Please keep this book close to your work area and refer to it often. My dream is for every threadplayer to need a second copy because their first one is completely worn out.

Scatter Shot (detail)

The Basics

Firebrand (detail)

THREADS

*L*et me make it clear from the start—I love threads! Luscious rayons, smooth silks, sparkly metallics, glitzy tinsels, sturdy cottons, it doesn't matter. Each one has something to offer that is unique. We can piece with ultra-fine synthetics; quilt with variegated metallics; accent with fluorescents; or embellish with yarn, ribbon, or cording. This section will guide you through these exciting possibilities. I am sure there are threads not mentioned, but by all means, go ahead and try them (on a test piece first, please). A word of caution—always buy the best you can afford. Saving a few pennies in the beginning can cost you big time in the finished product.

In order to talk about thread, we need to know some terms:

Weight. In threadspeak, *weight* means fineness and is often abbreviated as "wt." Another term for thread weight is *denier* (DEN-year). Thread weight is indicated by numbers, which run anywhere from 12 to 100. The higher the number, the finer the thread. In other words, 30-weight thread is thicker than 40-weight.

Ply. A *ply* is a strand of thread. One-ply thread, often called *blending filament*, is very weak. Three-ply thread, or three strands twisted together, is much stronger. Always use three-ply thread for piecing seams.

A spool of thread may be labeled with a set of numbers, such as 50/3. This means it is 50-weight and 3-ply—the type used by quilters for general piecing.

Mercerized Cotton

The thread most often used by traditional quiltmakers is 100% mercerized cotton. It has been chemically treated with caustic soda to improve its luster and strength and to make it more receptive to dyes. Three-ply mercerized cotton is great for general piecing because it is strong, uniform, and durable. Mettler Silk-Finish, Gütermann, Signature, MasterPiece by Superior, and Aurifil are good brands. The threads in the bin with a "Ten Spools for $1" sign are not.

Pros: Comes in the largest assortment of colors and is the best choice for piecing cotton fabrics.

Cons: Mercerized cotton thread has no stretch, so don't use it when you need some "give." It also absorbs moisture, which can weaken thread over time.

Decorative Cotton

In addition to mercerized cotton sewing thread, there are a variety of decorative cotton threads. These unmercerized threads range from 12-weight to 80-weight. The most popular weights are 30 and 60, and they come in a wide selection of solid, shaded, and variegated colors. This soft, flexible thread fills in decorative stitches very well. Cotton threads used in embroidery have a matte finish. Good brands are Mettler, Oliver Twist, Superior King Tut, Valdani, and DMC.

Pros: Comes in the widest variety of weights.

Cons: There is a vast range in quality. Buyer beware!

Quilting

Thread made specifically for quilting is stronger and thicker than regular sewing thread. Be careful not to use threads marked "for hand quilting" in your sewing machine. The waxed coating can jam the tension discs and cause other disasters. Anchor, Gütermann, Mettler, Molnlycke, and Signature all make 100% cotton quilting thread. DMC offers a quilting thread that is a cotton-polyester blend.

Pros: Makes a very strong stitch.

Cons: Has a tendency to knot.

Rayon

Rayon threads are among my favorites. The most popular brands are Sulky and Madeira. Both companies offer 30-weight and 40-weight rayon threads in a wide range of colors, especially in the 40-weight. Madeira also makes fluorescent and neon colors, as does Janome. Other brands to look for are Coats & Clark, Finishing Touch, MegaSheen, Mez Alcazar, Natesh, Radiante, and YLI. Other brands may attract you, but be sure to test for colorfastness and uniformity.

PROS: Stitches have a lustrous look; fills in decorative stitches beautifully.

CONS: Thread is soft and subject to fading when washed. Do not use for construction purposes or anything that is washed frequently.

Acrylic

Ultrasheen by YLI is the only brand of acrylic thread currently on the market. It is similar to rayon thread in appearance, but is a little finer. I expect to see more brands in the near future.

Silk

Harder to find and more expensive than rayon, silk thread gives a glow to your work. It is a fine, yet strong, thread. Clover, Kanagawa and YLI brands are the most readily available in the United States. If you have friends going to Asia, suggest silk thread as a souvenir. You will love it, and they will have no trouble packing it!

PROS: Stronger and stretchier than cotton thread. Great for basting because it doesn't leave holes in the fabric.

CONS: Hard to find and expensive.

Metallic

Wonderfully decorative, metallic threads are made by wrapping metal thread around a core fiber. Sulky, Madeira, Superior, Yenmet, Signature, and YLI offer the most variety and best quality. Madeira metallics include Dazzle, Supertwist, and FS Jewel. Tire makes both 30-weight and a finer 50-weight in gold and silver. Kreinek metallic threads are good but are most widely available in small amounts packaged for hand sewing. If you plan to use Kreinek, be sure to check the amount of thread on each spool and buy enough.

To determine how a metallic thread will sew, cut off the end, unwrap a length, and run it between your thumb and forefinger. If it doesn't fray and feels smooth and even, you shouldn't have any problems. If it frizzes beyond recognition and feels like cut glass, don't even try to put it in the machine. If it falls somewhere in between, try lightly coating the thread on the spool with liquid silicone (see page 20).

PROS: Versatile and a great accent thread.

CONS: Can be tricky to use and tends to break.

Bobbin/Lingerie

Synthetic bobbin and lingerie threads (nylon or polyester) are great to use in the bobbin when you're working with decorative threads on the top, especially metallics. Metallic threads tend to be brittle. If you use cotton thread in the bobbin it will "grab" the metallic thread, causing it to break. Because bobbin and lingerie threads are very fine (60-weight to 90-weight) and smooth, they will not grab the metallic thread. I also like to use bobbin threads for piecing miniatures and wall pieces that will not get a lot of wear. My favorite is The Bottom Line by Superior Threads. This 60-wt. polyester thread is lint-free and comes in the biggest variety of colors. Tru-Sew by Coats & Clark, YLI Bobbin & Lingerie, and Metrolene by Mettler also work well although the color selection is limited.

PROS: Terrific for use in the bobbin when you're using decorative threads on top. You can wind a great deal of thread on a bobbin. Doesn't build up a lot of thread on the wrong side of the quilt.

CONS: Comes in very few colors. You may need to tighten the bobbin tension. See the illustration on page 66.

Monofilament

Monofilament thread is wonderful when you are sewing over a lot of different colored fabrics and don't want to change thread all the time. These translucent threads are very fine (size .004), yet strong, and they resemble ultrafine fishing line. I prefer the polyester monofilaments over the nylon or polyamide. Polyester has a much higher heat tolerance and doesn't get brittle over time. Sulky Invisible and Superior MonoPoly are good brands and come in smoke (for dark colors) and clear (for light colors).

PROS: Blends with any color.

CONS: Because the thread is hard to see, it can be hard to thread a needle. Try marking the tip of the thread with a black marker.

Tinsel

Similar to skinny Christmas tinsel, tinsel thread is a flat polyester filament with a highly reflective surface. Some tinsel threads are coated with aluminum and others actually have tiny holograms on their surfaces. Good brands include Glitter by Superior, Sliver and Holoshimmer by Sulky, and Laserbrite by Signature.

PROS: The shiniest thread available.

CONS: Does not fill in decorative stitches well. Sometimes it doesn't unwind evenly off the spool.

Topstitching

Heavy, tightly twisted topstitching threads are most often used for accenting a line or making buttonholes. They are also used for sashiko and edge stitching. Topstitching threads come in silk, polyester, cotton-covered polyester, and cotton. Good brands are Belding Corticelli, Gütermann, Tire, YLI Jeans Stitch, and Zwicky.

PROS: Creates a definite line.

CONS: Hard to find and calls for a large needle.

Polyester

While I don't recommend piecing cotton quilt fabrics with polyester thread, I love it for decorative stitching. Polyester threads can be spun, filament or trilobal. These terms describe the manufacturing processes and all produce quality threads. The most common sizes for decorative stitching are 30- and 40-weight. High-quality polyester threads are lint-free and colorfast. They also have a very high melting point, making them heat resistant. These factors make them my decorative threads of choice for any project that will be washed and/or ironed frequently. They also come in many colors, including variegated, neons, and ombres. There are lots of good brands, including Isacord, Superior, Sulky, Mettler, Madeira, Robison-Anton, and YLI.

PROS: Resistant to heat, stretching and shrinking. Lintfree and colorfast.

CONS: None.

Decorative

Some threads are too thick to go through a size 90/14 machine needle. You might be able to thread them through a 100/16 needle, but the needle would make a large hole in the fabric. I prefer to wind thick threads on the bobbin and sew from the reverse side. For these threads to work in the bobbin, they must be fairly smooth and even, with no "nubbies." See "Bobbin Drawing" on page 66.

Smooth threads include Madeira Decor, YLI Designer 6, ArtFloss 6, pearl cotton, and Pearl Crown Rayon. They come wound on a spool. Artfabrik also hand dyes some beautiful pearl cotton threads. Some thick threads are sold in skeins or on cards. To prevent tangling, wind these threads onto an empty spool before loading a bobbin.

Metallic threads include Madeira Glamour, YLI Candlelight, Razzle Dazzle by Superior, and Kreinik Braids (sizes 8, 12, and 16). There are other thick metallic threads, but the ones I have tried are too uneven to go through the bobbin tension.

PROS: Creates a thick line. Changing directions and making curves with thick threads is much easier when you use them in the bobbin than when you couch them.

CONS: Because the thread is thick, you can't get much of it on the bobbin. Do not use with dense decorative stitches unless you adjust the stitch for the thickness of the thread.

Trims and Ribbons

Anything that is too thick to thread through a needle and too uneven to go through the bobbin must be stitched to the surface. This includes wide ribbons, braids, cords, sequins, cross-locked beads, and textured yarns. See "Couching" on page 71.

PROS: Adds texture and emphasis to your work.

CONS: Finishing the ends of trims and ribbons can be tricky.

FABRICS

If you think there are a lot of threads to choose from, just wait until you look at fabrics! Today's quiltmakers are blessed with an almost unlimited fabric palette. Everything from the sheerest silk organza to the heaviest cotton duck canvas can be and has been used in art quilts. After some experimentation, I have narrowed my fabric choices to those that are particularly suited to threadplay and quilts. In this section I will focus on the fabrics I have found to be effective in my own quilts.

When I first began to make quilts, I would buy one to six yards of each fabric. Then I realized that all my quilts looked alike. Now I usually buy ¼- to ½-yard pieces and use them up. I buy one or two yards of large-scale prints and five to ten yards for quilt backs.

Commercial Cottons

The traditional fabric for quiltmaking is 100% cotton. It comes in widths from 36" to 60". Many reliable manufacturers are doing their best to entice us with their prints, solids, stripes, florals, and geometrics. I consider it my duty as a quiltmaker, teacher, consumer, and loyal citizen to buy as many of them as possible! There is some truth in that last statement. Let me explain. Each season, manufacturers choose a different selection of colors to print. One year it may be blue-greens and the next it will be yellow-greens. If you need an olive green and it's a blue-green year, you may be out of luck. Try to keep at least a mental inventory of which colors you need.

I prewash all my cotton fabrics using a small amount of detergent, warm water, and a regular wash cycle. Since I sell my quilts, I want to make them as sturdy as possible. If a fabric fades or changes too much in the wash, I don't use it in my quilts. If you worry about bleeding, try a commercial color inhibitor (Retayne and Color Shield are two brand names). When I first began to make art quilts, I tried to use some sleazy fabrics and was always sorry. If you are going to invest the time and effort it takes to make a quilt, invest in good fabrics.

Hand-Dyed Cottons

I love the subtlety of hand-dyed fabrics but have no desire to dye them myself. Part of the reason quiltmaking first appealed to me was that it did not smell and my hands stayed dry—the antithesis of dyeing. I happily support the dyers of the world; their product is excellent.

Cotton-Polyester Blends

While purists denounce the use of blends, I have used them in certain cases without any problems. In general, the more cotton in the blend, the better it will work. Remember that 100% polyesters can cause bearding (the batting works its way through the fabric and appears as threads or pills on top).

Sheers

Included in the sheer category are netting, voile, chiffon, gauze, tulle, and organza. These fabrics are too delicate to be used alone in most quilts, but they are great for creating shadows and softening edges. See *Outback Rain* on page 92.

Frenzy (detail)

ORGANIZATION AND STORAGE

Fabric

I keep my fabric in a modular storage system consisting of plastic-covered wire units. This kind of system offers so many components that you can customize it to fit whatever space you have. If you store your fabrics in a modular basket setup, make sure you use baskets of a moderate size. If your baskets are too big, they become so heavy when you load them with fabric that you can't slide them out easily. Between two of the units, I have shelves where I store fabric for quilt backs.

I try to organize my fabrics according to type and color. For instance, I have baskets marked "medium red solids," "green prints," and "small stripes." I keep my hand-dyed fabrics in a separate unit.

Thread

I'm not sure if I have more fabric or threads! Luckily, threads are a little easier to store as they don't take up as much room. I use a variety of storage methods. My metallics sit on shelves meant to hold miniatures that are mounted in the hallway outside the entrance to my studio. Solid rayons are in Sulky Slimline Storage Boxes which I unhooked and mounted on my studio wall. All the others are in vertical cabinets sorted by type and color. No matter what system you use, be sure to keep all threads out of direct sunlight.

Part of the problem with storing threads is keeping the thread tails in place. For thread spools that don't have a catch to hold the thread end, I cut clear-plastic tablecloth material into 1½" or 2" lengths or I use Hugo's Amazing Tape. I cut a strip and then wrap it around the spool with a little overlap. To make the end of the strip easier to see, I cut it at an angle and draw an arrow on it with a permanent marker.

Notions

I like my notions out where I can see them. I have read all about how to construct a pegboard wall, and it sounds great. However, I use a different system. Whenever I need to store a notion, I get out a nail of the appropriate size and hammer it into the wall. Works every time! I try not to use monster nails so the holes won't be too big.

I keep notions that are too small to put on a nail in little tool cabinets or in baskets that line my windowsill. All my hoops hang in the hall along with my thread.

Haywire (detail)

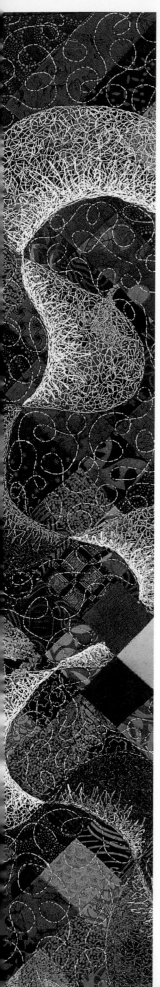

SEWING MACHINES

Machines

The most important and expensive part of threadplay is the sewing machine. The key factors that determine success are the abilities of the machine, the abilities of the operator (you), and how well the operator knows the machine.

What machine is best? That's a hard question. I'll give you the same advice I got about buying a computer: Find out what you will use the machine for, then buy the one that performs those functions. I must say that this advice was no help at all to me. If I didn't know what each machine's possibilities were, how could I know which to choose? My advice to you is to talk to other quiltmakers who have figured out what they are doing, sift through their counsel, and then face the salesperson.

Do buy the best machine you can afford. Today's computerized machines make threadplay a real pleasure. Another factor to consider is the dealership in your area. Does it offer service and support? Does it carry the full line of presser feet and accessories? Do you like the feel of the store? What are the store hours? When I teach, I can always tell which dealership in the area is the most user friendly because the majority of students own the same brand of machine. You can also check with *Consumer Reports* and the local Better Business Bureau.

What features should your machine have? No machine has all the features ever invented. Personally, I love Bernina machines. I use the Bernina artista 200 because it offers a wide (9mm) satin stitch, directional sewing, a securing stitch, eleven needle positions, a needle-down option, and Bernina's patented knee-operated presser foot lifter. I also have several of the aurora series as backups. Other threadplayers are just as avid about their particular machine brand and model. It really is a matter of personal and financial choice.

No matter what type of machine you have or what type of sewing you do, you will sew better if you know your machine. Before you do anything else, get out that owner's manual and read it. You won't be sorry!

Accessory Feet

Today's machines have accessory feet for every conceivable technique and circumstance. Here is a list of the feet I find especially helpful for threadplay.

Darning: Use this foot for free-motion stitching. Some darning feet are closed, some are open. Some are made of metal, some of clear plastic. When you put the darning foot on your machine and lower the presser bar, the foot will not touch the throatplate. Don't worry. This is normal and is what allows you to move the fabric freely.

Darning foot

Quilting or Big Foot: Most machines now make a specific foot for free motion quilting. Bernina has several, including a new patented stitch regulator (see page 79).

Open-Toe Embroidery: If you are not sure which foot to use for embroidery, turn some over and look for one with a wide groove on the bottom. This groove lets the presser foot ride over heavy or wide stitching. The open toe allows you to see your work as you stitch.

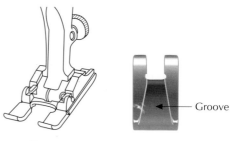

Open-toe
embroidery foot

— Groove

Child's Play (detail)

Braiding: The braiding foot is similar to the open-toe embroidery foot except there is a bar across the front with a hole in the middle of it. Some machines offer two braiding feet, one with a large hole and the other with a small hole, to accommodate different sizes of threads or trims.

Patchwork or Little Foot: The right edge of this foot is exactly ¼" from the needle when the needle is in the center position. There are also marks that let you know when the needle is ¼" from the end of a seam whether you are sewing backward or forward.

Piping or Bulky Overlock: The groove on the bottom of this foot is large and rounded to accommodate fat trims up to ¼" thick.

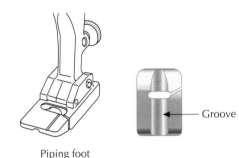

Braiding foot

Piping foot

Groove

Child's Play

by Libby Lehman, 1995, Houston, Texas, 22" x 27". Collection of Cindy Gray.

MACHINE NEEDLES

*S*ewing-machine needles are made up of six parts.

Shank: The part of the needle that fits into the machine. The shanks of modern machine needles have flat backs. Make sure you insert the needle with the rounded side facing you. If you have an old machine, ask for a round-shank needle.

Shaft: The body of the needle.

Groove: An indentation on the front of the shaft. The groove acts as a tunnel for the thread to ride in as the needle penetrates the fabric.

Scarf: An indentation on the back of the shaft just above the eye. When the bobbin hook rises up to the needle, it passes through the scarf, catching a loop of thread on the way down. This is what makes a stitch.

Eye: The hole through which the thread passes. The eye must be large enough to accommodate the thread without causing wear.

Point: The sharp end of the needle.

Singer and Schmetz manufacture the majority of machine needles. Use Singer needles with Singer and Kenmore machines; use Schmetz needles with European machines. Schmetz also makes needles for Elna and Bernina that are sold under their names. Consult your machine's manual if you are not sure what brand of needle fits your machine.

Schmetz packages their needles in sets of five. At the top of the plastic pack are rounded areas that magnify the shank. Etched in the shank is the needle size. If you have eagle eyes or if the light is just right, you may be able to read it. I keep a lighted magnifier handy. Sometimes you can find a dealer who buys needles in bulk and sells them individually. These needles will be cheaper, since you are not paying for the packaging.

Before I discovered quiltmaking, I never knew that needles dulled with use. I only changed the needle when it broke (sometimes a matter of years). Now I change needles after every eight hours worth of sewing at least. A sharp new needle makes a world of difference in the final product.

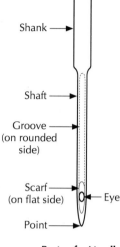

Shank —→
Shaft —→
Groove —→
(on rounded side)
Scarf —→
(on flat side) —← Eye
Point—→

Parts of a Needle

Using a variety of needles can be confusing. I try to put a Post-it note on the machine telling me what needle is in it. A handy way to organize used, but still good, needles is a tomato-style pincushion. Mark each wedge with a needle description ("T" for Topstitch, "E" for Embroidery, and so on). You can subdivide each wedge into different sizes. Simply stick the needle in the proper section when changing to a different needle. You can also stick a bright-colored straight pin in the appropriate pincushion section to show which needle is in the machine.

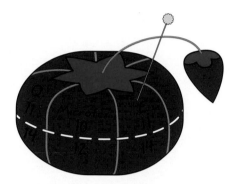

The pin means you have an embroidery needle, size 11, in the machine.

Sizes

Sewing machine needles are sized according to the diameter of the shaft. There are two numbering systems: European and American. European sizing is based on the shaft size in hundredths of a millimeter, from 60 to 120. American sizing uses an arbitrary number from 8 to 21. Both the European and American sizes are shown on most needles as follows: 60/8, 65/9, 70/10, 75/11, 80/12, 90/14, 100/16, 110/18, and 120/20. In either system, the larger the number, the bigger the needle. Needles for hand sewing are numbered in the opposite manner.

Points

In addition to size, needles are grouped according to the type of point. Singer needles are color-coded. Use red-band needles for piecing woven fabrics and yellow-band needles for decorative stitching. Schmetz needles sometimes have the designation 130/705H; the "H" stands for hohlkehle ("long scarf" in German).

Universal: This is the most widely available needle. Its slightly rounded point works well with a majority of fabrics. However, I never use it. It is sort of like "one size fits all"; it does a bunch of jobs fairly well, but it is not the best needle for anything.

H-J or Jeans/Denim: Designed to sew densely woven fabrics, this needle has a very sharp point, stiff shaft, and narrow eye. Schmetz marks theirs with a blue band on the shank.

H-M or Microtex Sharp: Very similar to the Jeans/Denim needle, this type was developed for use with microfiber fabrics. It has a very sharp point and a narrow eye. Schmetz marks theirs with a purple band on the shank. Lammertz also makes this needle.

130N or Topstitching: The eye is very large and the groove is deeper than the Universal needle. These features help to keep the thread from fraying. The large eye makes the needle somewhat weak, but I have no problem sewing through quilt-weight fabrics or quilting with it.

H-E or Embroidery: Designed for decorative machine stitching, this needle is currently available only in assortment packs of three 75/11s and two 90/14s. It is marked with a red band.

H-MET or Metallica: Schmetz makes this 80/12 needle designed for metallic and tinsel threads. It has a large eye that has been treated to reduce friction, a long scarf, and a deep groove.

H-M or Metalfil: Lammertz treats this 80/12 needle with an alloy that withstands the higher temperatures caused by metallic-thread friction. Its specialized eye and scarf are designed to prevent metallic threads from fraying.

H-Q or Quilting: Developed specifically for piecing and quilting, this needle has a sharp, tapered point and is marked with a green band. It is sold in assortment packs of three 75/11s and two 90/14s.

Special-Purpose Needles

Spring: If your machine does not have a darning foot, look into this needle. It is an 80/12 Universal needle with a wire spring around it. The spring acts much like a darning foot. You can replace the needle inside the spring if you are careful. I tried replacing one with a 90/14 Topstitching needle. It worked, but the bigger shaft made a noise like a donkey braying as it rubbed against the plastic parts at the spring ends!

Self-Threading: Available in sizes 80/12 and 90/14, this needle has a small slit on one side that makes it easy to thread. Self-threading needles are fragile; sew slowly and don't pull the fabric.

Multiple Needles

Multiple needles are easy to identify because there are two or more needles attached to the same shank by a crossbar. The numbering system is a little different. The first number is the distance between the needles in millimeters and the second number is the European size. A 1.6/70 twin needle has two size 70 needles that are 1.6mm apart. These needles can be used only in a front-threading zigzag machine. A straight-stitch machine can't accommodate the width of multiple needles.

H-ZWI, Twin or Double: Available with Stretch, Jeans, Metallica, or Embroidery needles, this type has two needles mounted on a crossbar.

H-DRI, Drilling or Triple: This type has three needles mounted on a crossbar. Be sure your throatplate can accommodate the stitch width.

Needles for Nontraditional Fabrics

In addition to the needles listed previously, there are several needles made for fabrics not traditionally used in quiltmaking. I am including them for the more adventurous among you.

H-LL, H-R, NTW, or Leather: The sharp, wedge-shaped point penetrates leather very well. Do not use with regular fabric because it will shred it to pieces.

H-S or Stretch: This blue needle has a slightly more rounded point than the Universal needle. Instead of penetrating fibers, it pushes them aside. Made for sewing slinky knits, synthetic leathers, and suedes.

H-SES, H-SUK, or Ballpoint: The Ballpoint has the roundest tip of any needle. The round tip allows it to pass between knitted fibers. Marked with a copper band. Use these needles for any knitted fabric.

Wing: These large needles (sizes 100/16 and 120/20) have metal flanges on each side of the shaft that act as hole punchers. They are used for decorative hemstitching and heirloom sewing.

ZWIHO or Double Hemstitch: This is a double needle with a wing needle on the left and a Universal needle on the right; use it for decorative and heirloom stitching.

Needle Selection

After reading the above you may feel ready to throw in the towel. Don't give up! Choosing a needle really isn't as complicated as it sounds. Ideally, you want to use the smallest needle possible and the appropriate point for the job. Here are the needles I use, found after a lot of trial and error.

Jeans/Denim 70/10 or 80/12: I use one of these needles for piecing instead of a Universal 80/12. The sharp point makes the straightest possible stitch and the small shaft doesn't make big holes. The 70/10 may be a little hard to thread and is not quite as strong as the 80/12, but it pieces cottons like a dream. If you can't find a Jeans/Denim needle, look for a 70/10 or 80/12 Microtex needle, which is similar.

Topstitching 90/14: The Topstitching needle is my favorite for stitching and quilting with metallic threads. It has a bigger eye than the Metalfil and Metallica needles and is more readily available. The Metalfil and Metallica are also good and are getting easier to find.

Embroidery 75/11 or 90/14: Embroidery needles are great with 40-weight rayons because the eye is large and the point is sharp. Actually, most rayon threads are soft and not particular about which needle they like best.

Tinderbox

by Libby Lehman, 1993, Houston, Texas, 46" x 46". Collection of Maurine Noble.

MACHINE PREPARATION

Cleaning and Oiling the Machine

Before you do any sewing, you need to clean your machine. We're not talking a light going over, we're talking clean! I clean my machine every time I change the bobbin. Think of it as taking a bath. How would you like to go for days without one, much less months? It is amazing how much lint and other grunge can accumulate in a short time. Do yourself and that wonderful machine a favor, and get in the habit of cleaning it often.

Supplies: Lightweight machine oil, several cotton swabs, a craft pipe cleaner or chenille stem.

1. Unplug the machine. I'm ashamed to admit that I don't always do this. If you leave the machine on, be sure to take your foot off the pedal.

2. Remove the presser foot, lower the feed dogs if possible, and remove the throatplate. You can also remove the needle just to be safe.

3. Remove the bobbin case, referring to your sewing machine manual. Remove the hook if it is easy to do so. Put a few drops of lightweight oil on the end of a cotton swab. Be sure it is lightweight oil, especially if you have an upper-end machine. If your manual says not to oil the machine, you can use a little denatured alcohol instead. The oil or alcohol acts as a dust magnet and keeps the cotton swab from disintegrating. You can also use a brush, but I like the convenience of tossing the swab when I'm through.

Trip Around the World: Bon Voyage

by Libby Lehman, 1991, Houston, Texas, 70" x 84". Collection of Lynda Milligan and Nancy Smith.

4. Clean the bobbin and throatplate areas with the swab. If you haven't done this in awhile, it may take several swabs. Gently poke the swab into any holes you can see. Don't force it—the key word is "gently." Clean the bobbin-case interior, the throatplate, and the hook with the swab.

5. Use the pipe cleaner to clean the slots between the feed dogs.

6. Check around the take-up lever to make sure no loose thread ends are caught. If so, clean them out by flossing with a polyester thread or using tweezers.

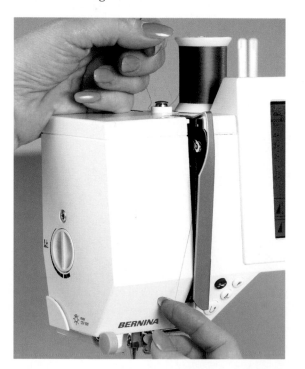

7. Oil the machine according to your manual, then reassemble the machine.

8. Stitch through a scrap of fabric to absorb any excess oil. If you think cleaning and oiling is not a necessity, just listen to that machine purr!

Machine Setup

Most of the stitching used in threadplay is either straight stitching or free-motion stitching. I'll give you precise setups for each technique, but here are some general guidelines.

STRAIGHT STITCHING

Check to see that the top tension is at its normal setting. Use a 70/10 or 80/12 Microtex or Jeans/Denim needle when working with regular-weight cotton fabrics and cotton thread. These needles have a very sharp point and make an excellent straight stitch. Use a ¼"-wide seam allowance unless instructed otherwise.

FREE-MOTION STITCHING

Lower the feed dogs. If your machine does not have this capability, cover them by taping a piece of index card over the opening. Cut a small opening in the card to accommodate the needle. Use a free-motion foot, such as a darning foot. You will probably have to lower the top tension. When you are feeding the fabric rather than letting the feed dogs do it, there is more drag on the top thread.

Make any adjustments your machine requires for free-motion sewing; presser-foot tension, half-step presser foot lifter, and so on. Refer to your sewing-machine manual.

METALLIC THREADS

Metallic threads give a wonderful twinkle to your work. They love to play the starring role. Sometimes, however, they also demand star treatment. If you've ever tried to sew with metallic threads, the first thing you probably discovered is that they get huffy and tend to fray and break. There are several things you can do to calm them down.

- Lower the top tension.
- Use a #14 Topstitch needle or one of the new needles made especially for metallics. If you have the right needle but have been sewing with it for awhile, replace it.
- Do not use the last thread guide. This is the one just before the needle. It is a tight fit and can cause the thread to fray. If your machine has a built-in needle threader, thread this guide, thread the needle, and then take the thread out of the last guide.
- Try using liquid silicone on the thread. Hold the spool horizontally and run a thin bead of silicone from one end to the other. Rotate the spool and repeat three or four times. Don't overdo it— too much liquid silicone can gum up the tension discs. Do not use on tinsel or monofilament threads— they do not absorb silicone.
- Use bobbin or lingerie thread in the bobbin. These slick threads won't try to grab the metallic thread the way a fuzzy cotton or cotton-covered polyester thread will.

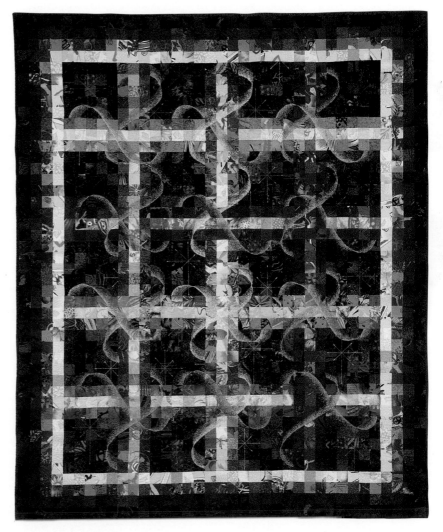

Sheer Rhapsody

by Libby Lehman, 1992,
Houston, Texas, 72" x 88".

TOOLS

I don't know a quilter who is not crazy about gadgets. I love to shop in hardware, sporting goods, office supply, and wholesale florist stores. Any place filled with gizmos gets my attention (there is a police officer's supply store I'm itching to visit). In this section, I will try to curb my enthusiasm and limit the discussion to items I find especially helpful in threadplay. I'll cover their particular uses in the appropriate technique section.

Scissors

CURVED-POINT SCISSORS

My son is an expert fly fisherman who ties custom flies. My favorite snips are a small pair of curved-point scissors that he gave me. Since they are intended for men, the finger holes are large, unlike most curved-point scissors. I can leave these scissors on my hand for frequent snipping or put them on the bobbin winder for quick access. The curved point allows me to clip threads right next to the fabric as I stitch, without cutting the fabric.

APPLIQUÉ SCISSORS

I prefer the appliqué scissors without the flange because I am left-handed. These scissors cut horizontally and are very sharp. Mundial and Gingher make them.

Sewing Problem Solvers

Liquid silicone helps keep thread from breaking. To use, run a line of silicone down the length of your thread spool in several places. The silicone will be absorbed by the thread. Do not use too much; it can gum up the tension discs. Also, do not use on tinsel or monofilament threads—they don't absorb silicone.

Needle threaders and **large-eye hand-sewing needles** come in handy when I'm bobbin drawing. I use them to bring thick thread ends to the back of the fabric. Cotton-darning and silk-ribbon needles work well. Your needle threader should be sturdy; my favorite is made by LoRan.

Traction aids help you move the fabric under the needle. I use $1\frac{1}{2}$" rubber circles sold as Needle Grabbers. Just put them on the quilt top under your fingers for extra traction. You might also try Quilt Sew Easy hoops, which are horseshoe-shaped plastic hoops with handles on top and rubber on the bottom. Simply place the open end of the hoop around the needle and use the handles to manuever your quilt top. Sold as a set, the two hoops can be used independently or nested to aid in threadplay. See the photo on page 82.

Basting Accessories

Basting guns are similar to the machine used to put tags on clothing.

Safety pins, size 1 nickel or brass, are also great for basting.

A pin closer is essentially a dowel with a screw on the end; Kwik Klip and Pin Popper are two brand names: Use this tool to open and close pins when you safety-pin baste.

Spray adhesives are a new way to baste. Applied to the wrong side of the quilt top, spray adhesive provides a repositionable, pressure-sensitive bond. This is the way I now baste my quilts.

Thread Holders

Sometimes a spool of thread will "puddle" off the end. I have tried a lot of different gadgets meant to keep thread on spools; the following ones have worked best for me:

• If your spindle is vertical, get a horizontal spool holder. These are available for sergers, but they fit most sewing machines as well.

I tape a safety pin, small end up, on my machine near the thread spool; I use the pin as a thread guide. Place the spool on the horizontal spindle so that the thread feeds from the top, through the safety pin, then through the normal guides.

• Use a container that will let the thread plop around on its own. Place it behind the machine so it will not get tangled in the flywheel. The container must be big enough to hold the spool horizontally.

Horizontal thread holders are also helpful when you're stitching with a large spool or with a spool that has a cardboard core. The horizontal position helps the thread to feed evenly and prevents it from tangling around the cardboard core or spindle. They are usually sold two to a pack. Some machines come with a horizontal feed spindle, which makes horizontal thread holders unnecessary.

Haywire

by Libby Lehman, 1995, Houston, Texas, 48" x 36".

STABILIZERS

One of the first things you will notice when you do threadplay is that fabric tends to pucker when you don't you stabilize it. The most common stabilizing methods are described below. In each of the technique sections I will tell you which stabilizer to use with that particular method.

Embroidery Hoops

Embroidery hoops are made up of an outer ring and an inner one. They are made of wood or of plastic, and they come in two basic types: screw and spring. Hoops come in many sizes; the size of the hoop is the diameter of the circle. I use 6", 8", and 10" hoops. Anything smaller and you will constantly be moving the hoop around the fabric. Anything larger and you can't move the hoop freely under the arm of the machine. There are also some nifty shapes (oblong, square, and oval) if you want to go whole hog.

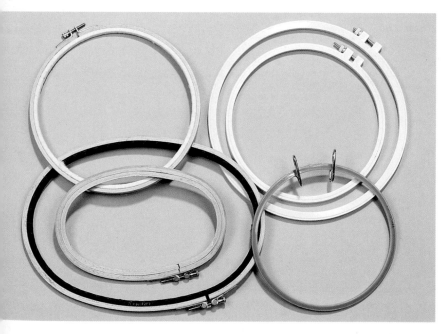

SCREW HOOPS

Screw embroidery hoops have a solid inner ring and an adjustable screw assembly on the outer ring. By tightening or loosening the screw, you can adjust the tension on the fabric in the hoop.

Wooden Hand-Embroidery Hoops

These hoops are inexpensive and readily available at craft stores. However, they do not work well for machine embroidery. They are too tall to pass under the needle easily. Also, the screw assembly is made of thin metal, which can bend.

Wooden Machine-Embroidery Hoops

I prefer wooden hoops made for machine embroidery. You can find wooden machine-embroidery hoops at most sewing machine dealers. They look like hand hoops, but look a little closer. For one thing, they will be more expensive ($8 to $20 instead of $1 to $5). Place a hand hoop and a machine hoop flat on a table. The machine hoop is shorter, which allows it to pass under the needle. Some hoops have a groove on one side of both rings to make it even easier to pass them under the needle. (be sure to line up the two grooves). The machine hoop is also much thicker, thus stronger. Look at the hardware. The screw on the machine hoop is at least twice as heavy as the one on the hand hoop. When you tighten the screw on the hand hoop as much as possible, it bends, causing you to lose tension. Unlike the hand hoop, the machine-hoop screw has a slot in the end so you can tighten it with a screwdriver.

Pick up the machine hoop and look at how the rings fit together. There should be no gaps between the inner and outer rings. You can make up for a small gap by wrapping the inner ring with twill tape, bias tape, or even old nylons. Wrapping also increases the tension and helps hold your fabric taut. Be sure to wrap evenly and sew or glue the end on the inside of the ring rather than the edge that touches the outer ring.

If you have done hand work in a hoop but not machine work, pay attention now. Getting the fabric in the machine hoop correctly is the opposite from hand embroidery. The fabric must be taut across the bottom of the hoop, not the top. To get the correct tension, loosen the tension to separate the inner and outer rings. Place the outer ring on a flat surface, then lay the fabric on top, right side up. Insert the inner ring and tighten the tension screw. Turn the assembled hoop over and pull the fabric taut. By pulling from the back side, you can avoid popping the fabric out on that last tug. Tighten the screw again until the fabric is like a drum. Be sure that the fabric is straight in the hoop and not distorted.

PROS: The best hoop for threadplay. Well made with great tension control and adjustability.

CONS: Expensive and may be hard to find.

PLASTIC MACHINE-EMBROIDERY HOOPS

Plastic machine-embroidery hoops are cheaper and more readily available than wooden ones. Susan Bates is a popular brand. These hoops have more give than the wooden ones, but they're still acceptable for two reasons. First, the screw is strong and easy to adjust. Second, the inner ring has a ridge that helps keep the fabric flat across the bottom of the hoop.

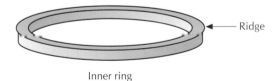

Inner ring — Ridge

To prepare, place the outer ring on a flat surface and the fabric on top of it, right side up. Turn the inner ring so the ridge faces down (ignore the printing on the ridge that says "this side up"). Push the inner ring through the outer one until the ridge is beyond the outer ring. Tighten the screw, turn the whole thing over, and pull the fabric taut. The ridge acts as a barrier to keep the fabric flat against the bed of the machine. There is also a hoop that has the ridge in the middle of the inner hoop. The ridge lines up with a corresponding groove on the inside of the outer hoop to keep the fabric taut and in place.

PROS: Inexpensive and easy to find at discount and craft stores.

CONS: Flexible with a lot of give.

SPRING HOOPS

Spring hoops consist of an outer plastic ring and an inner metal ring with handles at each end. They work well for techniques that don't cause a lot of puckering. To prepare for stitching, squeeze the handles together to remove the inner ring, place the fabric over the plastic outer hoop, and insert the metal ring in the groove of the outer ring.

PROS: Easy to use and to get under the needle.

CONS: You cannot control the tension.

Removable Stabilizers

Embroidery hoops provide the most support, but moving them around a quilt top can be frustrating. An alternative for some techniques is a tearaway stabilizer. Tearaway stabilizers are especially useful when you are doing satin or other straight-line stitching, because the stitching perforates the paper and makes it easy to tear. If you do free-motion work, it is much harder, if not impossible, to remove the paper after stitching, since you are stabbing the stabilizer in a random pattern, not in a straight line. I have used a tearaway stabilizer for free-motion work, but it required tweezers, a spray water bottle, and lots of patience to remove it.

PAPER

The simplest stabilizer is a piece of paper placed under your fabric. This works fine for small areas, such as a few bars of satin stitching. You just slip the paper under the fabric as you begin to stitch. Adding-machine tape is great for this. Tissue, deli, and tracing paper also work well.

PROS: Cheap and widely available.

CONS: For large areas, you have to pin the paper to the fabric. Some papers can dull the needle. Heavy paper can be hard to remove, and thin paper can tear before you finish stitching.

FREEZER PAPER

Freezer paper is the most commonly used tearaway stabilizer in the United States. One side has a slick, shiny coating that temporarily adheres to fabric when heated. To use, simply press the coated side to the wrong side of the fabric with a warm iron.

PROS: Inexpensive and readily available in the United States.

CONS: Somewhat stiff for large projects. Expensive outside the United States.

TEARAWAYS

Tearaway stabilizers are specially designed to tear out after stitching. Be careful to avoid pulling the stitches out of shape. If your project is large, you will need to pin or baste the tearaway stabilizer to your fabric. Try to match the weight of your stabilizer to your fabric. Brand names are Sulky Tear Easy, Stitch & Ditch, Stitch & Tear, and No Whiskers Tear Away.

PROS: Come in the widest variety of weights and sizes.

CONS: Can shift if not pinned carefully to the fabric.

Iron-on Stabilizers

Iron-on tearaway stabilizers are similar to freezer paper, but they have a softer hand. This softness makes the stabilizer easy to handle, particularly when you're trying to get large projects under the needle. Iron-on tearaway stabilizers are available in precut sheets, by the yard, or by the roll. They also come in different weights. Brands include Sulky Totally Stable, Jiffy Tear, and Press-N-Tear.

PROS: Thinner and softer than freezer paper.

CONS: Can stick too much to the fabric if the iron is too hot. If this happens, spray the stabilizer with water and remove it with tweezers.

Water-Soluble Stabilizers

LIQUIDS

A recent innovation, liquid stabilizer is a favorite of mine. Liquid stabilizer is clear and about the consistency of honey. You only need to apply it to the area you are going to stitch. Since I usually have no idea where I'm going to stitch, I pour it out and smear it all over the surface of the quilt top. Be sure to look for a brand that rinses out. You can speed up the drying time by using a fan or hair dryer. Press the quilt top after the liquid stabilizer dries, before stitching. To dissolve the stabilizer, rinse the stitched quilt top in hot water and let it dry. Perfect Sew and Lite Fabric Stiffener are the two brands I use. Lite Fabric Stiffener is available in both applicator and spray bottles.

Starch is another alternative. Use the liquid type, but do not dilute according to the directions. Use either full or half-strength starch (add no water or add only half the recommended amount). I prefer the other liquid stabilizers because they cover more evenly and make the fabric stiffer. Hair gels also stiffen fabric, but they are alcohol-based and can affect the color of your quilt top or thread. I do not recommend them as stabilizers.

PROS: Easy to stitch, since you don't have to move a hoop or fool with another layer. Easy to remove.

CONS: A lot of stitches in close proximity (double satin stitching, for example) can perforate the stiffened fabric and cause it to tear. The most expensive stabilizer.

SHEETS

Water-soluble stabilizers are available in sheets, which makes them convenient. Just rinse away the stabilizer with water when you're done stitching. Water-soluble sheets work well in hoops. These are soft stabilizers, best suited for lightweight fabrics or for transferring traced designs. Sulky Solvy, HTC RinsAway, Melt Away, and YLI Solv-It are good brands.

PROS: Easy to use for transferring designs, such as monograms. Scraps can be dissolved to make a liquid stabilizer.

CONS: Easily affected by air. Dries out in arid climates and dissolves in humidity. Keep in a sealed plastic bag.

Iron-Away Stabilizers

If you don't want to tear, wash, or rinse away a stabilizer, how about ironing? Called "vanishing muslin" in Great Britain, iron-away stabilizers are open-weave fabrics with a low melting point. After stitching, place a hot, dry iron over the project. The stabilizer will turn brown, char, and scare the living daylights out of you. Don't panic. Unless the setting of your iron is too hot for the fabric and threads in your quilt top, it won't hurt them. Once the stabilizer is completely brown, you can brush or shake it away. Brand names include Sulky Heat-Away Brush Off, Michelle Pullen's Vanish-a-Way, and Hot Stuff!

PROS: Useful when you don't want to get the fabric wet. Provides a stable base for stitched lace.

CONS: Expensive. Be careful not to scorch your project. If your stitching is dense, the stabilizer under the stitching may eventually work its way out and appear as "whiskers."

Adhesive Stabilizers

Adhesive stabilizers were developed for hooped, computerized machine embroidery, but they can also be used for free-motion work. To use, peel off the release sheet and stick your fabric on top of the adhesive stabilizer. Stitch, then remove the stabilizer from the fabric. Brand names are Sulky Sticky and Stick-It-All.

PROS: Adheres easily and does not require heat, an advantage for fine fabrics.

CONS: Some of the sticky residue will remain inside the dense stitching.

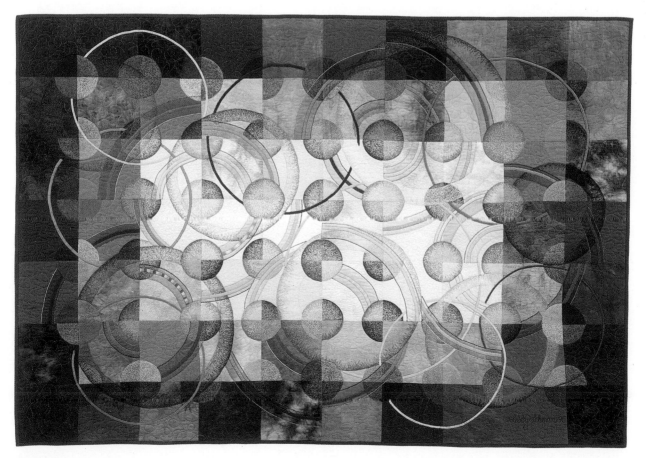

Rimshots

by Libby Lehman, 1995, Houston, Texas, 59" x 41". Collection of Donna Moog Nussbaum.

QUILT TOP CONSTRUCTION

*B*efore you can play with thread, you have to have a playground. You probably know how to piece a quilt top. I am only going to cover the two methods I use most often.

Chain Piecing Squares

I make a lot of my quilt tops from 2½" squares. I keep a library of precut squares, organized by color, in cardboard tie boxes.

Ribbon Weave

by Libby Lehman, 1996, Houston, Texas, 28" x 22". Collection of Loanne Hamje. *Chain-pieced background.*

One box is labeled "darks" and is filled with dark fabric squares in a variety of colors. I sew these dark squares together to make terrific backgrounds—the subtle color and texture changes add interest that I wouldn't get if I used only one fabric. I design my top by pinning squares to my work wall, one at a time. When I get to the outside edges, I switch from squares to 2½" x 3" rectangles, with 3" squares in the corners. This extra half inch is insurance. Quilting often draws up the fabric, making the outside edge ⅛" too short. It is much easier to trim off extra fabric than to add ⅛". I don't know why it took me so long to figure this out!

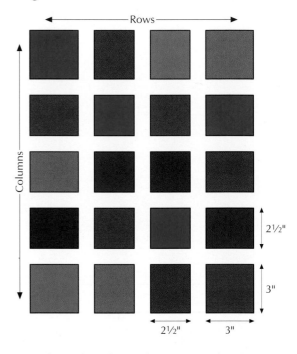

1. Stack each column from top to bottom.

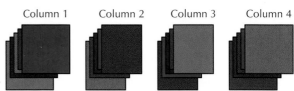

Column 1   Column 2   Column 3   Column 4

2. Place the first piece from column 2 on the first piece from column 1, right sides together. Stitch with a ¼"-wide seam allowance from end to end. Without lifting the presser foot, stitch the next pair. There will be a small area of stitching between each pair. Continue until you have stitched the pieces together from columns 1 and 2.

3. Do not cut the squares apart.

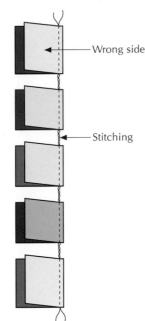

- Wrong side
- Stitching

4. Open the first stitched pair. Place the first piece from column 3 on top of the first piece from column 2, right sides together. Stitch column 3 to column 2, as you joined the columns in step 2. Continue adding pieces until you've added column 3 to the chain.

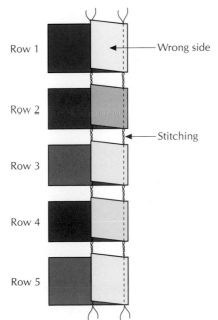

Row 1
Row 2
Row 3
Row 4
Row 5

- Wrong side
- Stitching

5. Continue until you've stitched all the columns together. There will be small areas of stitching between the columns.

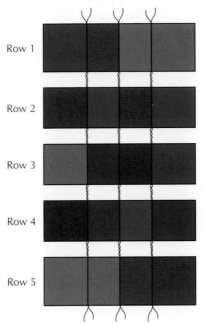

Row 1
Row 2
Row 3
Row 4
Row 5

6. Press the seams open or in alternating directions from row to row. Stitch the rows together. Press the seams open or to one side.

I love this method of chain piecing. Before I started doing it this way, I always got a square in backward or upside down, and it took forever to get back on track. With this method, the only thing to remember is which piece is the top left corner. I do this by placing a safety pin in it before I ever take the pieces off the wall.

Threadwinds

by Libby Lehman, 1993, Houston, Texas, 72" x 48". Collection of Bob and Linda Sherman. *Chain-pieced background.*

Crazy Piecing

If you want an irregular background, crazy piecing is the way to go. It's not necessarily a quick method, but the results are impressive. Begin by cutting some shapes out of fabric. I do this freehand with a rotary cutter. You can also use scraps left over from other projects.

Firebrand

by Libby Lehman, 1993, Houston, Texas, 40" x 40". Collection of Ursula Reikes. *Crazy-pieced background.*

1. Place two pieces right sides together, then stitch across them. The pieces do not have to line up. Press the seam to one side, then trim it to ¼". I call these units "two-fers." Make a bunch of them.

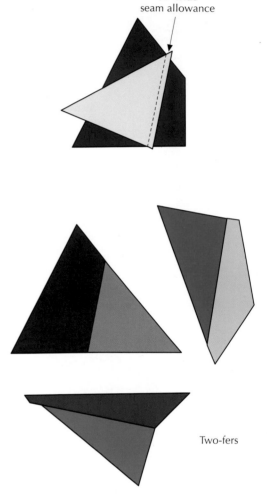

¼"-wide
seam allowance

Two-fers

2. Place 1 two-fer on top of another, right sides together. Rotary cut across both two-fers to get a straight edge.

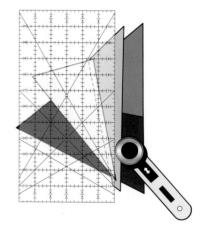

3. Stitch along the straight edge, using a ¼"-wide seam allowance. Press the seams to one side.

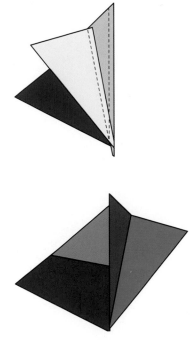

4. Keep adding two-fers to the edges of your piece. To make a two-fer longer, add another piece to one end. When you have a big piece, square it up.

Large tops are much easier to piece if you divide the top into sections, crazy piece the sections, and then sew the sections together.

STITCHING AN INSIDE CORNER

Think of crazy piecing as a jigsaw puzzle. The one thing you want to avoid is an inside corner. There are ways to piece inside corners, but they never work for me, so I developed the following method.

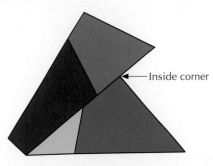

1. Place the piece to be added along the longest edge of the inside corner. Lower the needle at the corner intersection and stitch to the edge of the added piece.

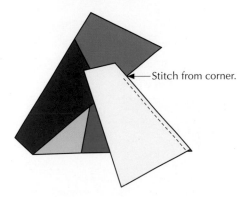

2. Flip the added piece to the right side and press. Turn the short edge under and blindstitch the inside corner with monofilament thread. This method guarantees a flat top.

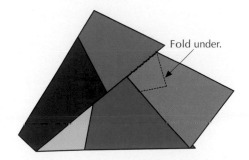

RIBBON ILLUSIONS

SHEER STITCHING

Threadplay Techniques

APPLIQUÉ

EMBROIDERY

RIBBON ILLUSIONS

I am crazy about ribbons. One of my closets is devoted to gift wrapping and includes a whole rack of assorted ribbons—metallic, satin, velvet, silk, curly—you name it, I've got it. It seemed only natural to stitch ribbons to my quilts, but I wanted to get a ribbonlike effect without using real ones. My first attempt was to quilt a ribbon design and fill it in with free-motion quilting. All this did was make the heavily quilted ribbon flat as a pancake, with about as much interest. After a lot of trial and error, I developed a way to stitch shaded, translucent ribbons on a pieced top and then quilt around them. Here's what you need and how to do it.

SUPPLIES: Quilt top, freezer paper or iron-on tearaway stabilizer, pencil, permanent marker, iron and ironing board, 8" or 10" machine-embroidery hoop, fine bobbin or lingerie thread, metallic sewing thread, 40-weight rayon thread in a coordinating light color.

The first thing you need to do is piece a top. Refer to "Quilt Top Construction" on pages 26–29 for more information. If you want to stitch metallic-thread ribbons, they will look better on a dark top than on a medium or light one. On my quilts, I like to use dark solids or muted prints with small accents of color.

Drawing the Ribbon

After you've pieced a top, you're ready to draw your ribbon. Cut a piece of freezer paper or iron-on tearaway stabilizer a little smaller than your top (2" to 4" smaller on each side). The smaller design will give you some leeway while ensuring that part of your ribbon doesn't end up in the seam allowance. If your top is wider than the paper, cut as many lengths of paper as needed and overlap them at the edges about 1", slick sides down, and press them together with a warm iron. Draw on the uncoated side.

CONTINUOUS RIBBON

1. Draw a big splat in the middle of your paper—this will not be a thing of beauty. Keep your curves fairly small. Mark the center of each straightaway, that is, each uncurved section of your design.

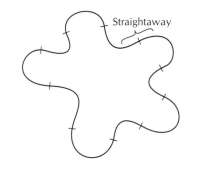
Straightaway

TIP

It is easier to draw large designs if you hold the pencil horizontally and move your entire arm instead of just your hand.

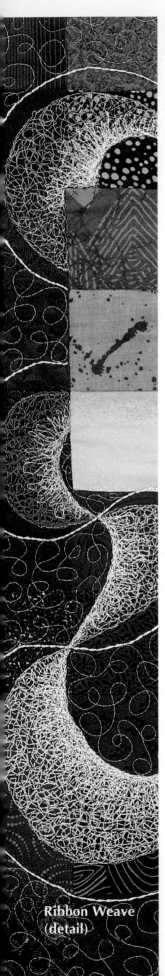

2. Starting at one of the center marks, draw a loop to the outside of your first splat. At the next mark, cross to the inside and make another loop.

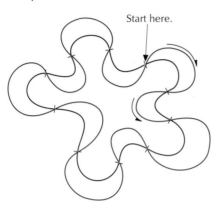

Start here.

It is important to draw your second line to the outside of whatever part of the first design sticks out the most. If you try to draw inside your first design, you will end up with the following:

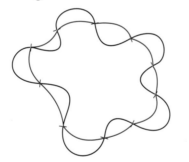

3. Continue until you have a complete ribbon. Go over your lines with a permanent marker, making corrections, if necessary, as you go.

STREAMERS

1. Draw as many curved lines as desired. Mark the center of each straightaway.

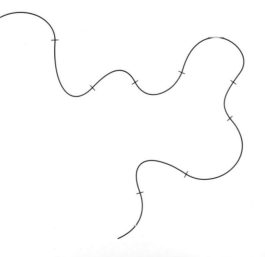

2. Draw a second line, curvier than the first, crossing over at each mark. For a natural look, I like to end each streamer with a "tail" rather than a point.

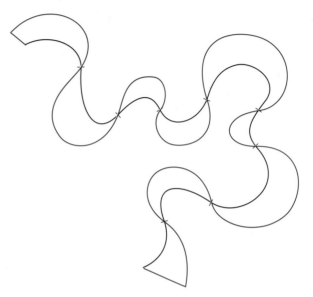

3. Go over your lines with a permanent marker, making corrections, if necessary, as you go.

TRACING A RIBBON

An alternative method suggested by a student is to draw several sizes of crescent shapes, including a tail. Place the tail shape on the piece of freezer paper and trace around it. Line up a crescent shape at the point of the tail and trace. Continue to alternate shapes as you trace each one. End by tracing the tail again.

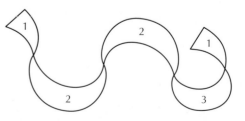

Transferring the Design

MACHINE SETUP FOR FREE-MOTION STITCHING	
Presser foot:	Darning (open or closed)
Needle: (choose one)	90/14 Topstitch, 90/14 Embroidery, 80/12 Metalfil, 80/12 Metallica
Needle position:	Down
Top thread:	Metallic or 40-weight rayon
Bobbin thread:	Bobbin/Lingerie
Top tension:	Loose
Feed dogs:	Down (or covered)
Stitch selection:	Straight
Stitch length:	N/A (in free-motion sewing, you determine this)
Stitch width:	N/A

1. Position the paper wherever you want on your quilt top. This maneuverability is one of the advantages of drawing on paper rather than directly on the fabric. Also, drawing on paper makes it much easier to correct mistakes. When the paper is in position, iron it to the right side of your quilt top with a warm, dry iron.

2. Set up your machine as directed in "Machine Setup." Position your quilt top under the needle somewhere along the ribbon line. Bring the bobbin thread to the top, through the fabric and paper.

3. Sew along the entire drawn figure with very small stitches. The stitches perforate the paper, and small stitches make removal easier. Remember that the feed dogs are at recess. You are now in charge of the stitch length.

To make small stitches, use a fast foot-pedal speed while moving your hands slowly. This will not come naturally. In fact, it will probably feel really awkward. Do not give up! Remember how much practice it took in third grade before you could write your name in cursive? Remember how proud you were when you finally did it? Here's your chance to experience that euphoria again. If you are a perfectionist, do a sample first. This is always good advice, but so is exercising regularly and brushing after every meal. You know your own levels of patience, confidence, and ability—act accordingly.

TIP

Stitching with metallic thread can be tricky. If you see the bobbin thread on the top, reduce the top tension by moving it to a lower number or toward the minus sign. Don't worry if it seems perilously low. The thread in the bobbin is very fine, and you are adding extra drag on the thread by pulling the hoop in different directions. Both these factors affect the tension balance. The tension controls work to create a balanced stitch. Unless you are at zero (you have to have some tension to sew), your machine doesn't really care where you set it.

4. After you have stitched over all the lines, it is time to tear away the paper. If the stitches are small and even, the paper will be perforated and will tear easily. If the stitches are less than ideal, hold the quilt top in one hand, right side up, and go over the stitched lines with the dull side of a seam ripper.

This will connect the dots the needle made and make it easier to tear the paper. You can leave paper on the ribbon sections if you want a preview of what it will look like, or if you want to make notes on these sections, such as color choices. I usually remove all the paper. You now have a permanent guideline that won't rub off or disappear in a few hours. Congratulations!

Stitching the Ribbon

1. Open the machine-embroidery hoop and put the larger hoop (the one with the screw assembly) on a flat surface. Place the quilt top, right side up, so at least one section of the ribbon is in the hoop. Fit the smaller hoop inside the outer one and push it until it rests ⅛" below the outer hoop. Tighten the screw. With the inner hoop ⅛" lower than the outer hoop, your fabric will stay flat against the bed of the machine.

Underside

⅛"

TIP

If you don't have a lot of hand strength, use a screwdriver in the screw slot.

---

2. Turn the hoop over. Pull on the quilt top until it is tight as a drum. Pulling from the back ensures that you won't pop the quilt top out of the hoop with that last tug. Make sure all the seams in the hoop are straight. If they are crooked and you stitch over them, they are crooked for life. Straighten them out now! Remove any remaining paper.

3. Thread your machine with your first color of decorative thread. I use metallic thread or 40-weight rayon. Place the hoop under the needle and lower the presser-foot lever. If you like to live dangerously, you can sew without a foot (known as sewing with a naked needle). I sew with a darning foot for two reasons. First, it makes it harder—not impossible, but harder—to sew through a finger. Second, it makes it easier to tell that the presser-foot lever is down.

4. Lower the top tension so that your stitches are loose. On Viking and Pfaff machines, you may have to go almost to "0." Berninas, New Homes, and Elnas range anywhere from 3½ to 1½.

5. Position the needle somewhere inside the first ribbon section. Bring the bobbin thread to the top. Take a few stitches almost in place to anchor the threads, then clip the ends. By not taking stitches right on top of each other, you will avoid making a lump. Fill in the ribbon section, using a straight or zigzag stitch. With a straight stitch, I make little loops, and with a zigzag, I sew in a random pattern. In either case, be sure to keep a loose grip on the hoop and move it in all directions. Stitching loops and random zigzags, along with using a foot, violate the ironclad rules of rigid machine embroidery, and I couldn't be more thrilled about it!

Straight (left) and zigzag (right) stitching

TIP

The advantage of a zigzag stitch is that the needle moves so you don't have to move the hoop quite as much. The disadvantage is that zigzag stitching increases the drag on your thread. You may have to lower the tension when using a zigzag stitch.

---

6. As you stitch, aim for an overall cobweb look. If you see the bobbin thread or notice some puckering, reduce the top tension. If you are almost at 0, try tightening the bobbin tension. You should be able to see some of the fabric through your stitching, but the density of your stitching depends on you. It is better to err on the side of too little stitching than to stitch too much and have to rip it out.

7. When you are through with one ribbon section, take a few anchoring stitches and clip the thread ends. Go to the next ribbon section, moving the hoop as needed.

Highlighting

After you have filled in a ribbon section, you will notice that it looks rather flat. In order to bring it to life, you need to add highlights. You can highlight each section as you go, or you can stitch all the sections and then add the highlights. It just depends on what you want to do less often—move the hoop or change threads.

1. Choose a new thread that is the same color as the previous stitching but a different value (lighter on a dark background, darker on a light background). If you used a variegated thread the first time, choose a second thread in whichever color is dominant. If you used metallic thread the first time, use rayon for this step; you have a wider selection of colors and there is less likelihood of breakage.

2. Stitch a second time, with either a straight or a zigzag stitch, along one edge of the section. This second pass should never extend more than half the width of the section. The idea is to blend the second thread into the first. You can highlight along either edge, but make your stitches feathery. You want to blend the colors rather than create distinct rows. It doesn't take a lot of stitching to get the desired effect. Again, less is more.

3. Continue until you have highlighted all the sections. Remove the hoop and admire.

Highlighting along the outer edge accentuates the curve.

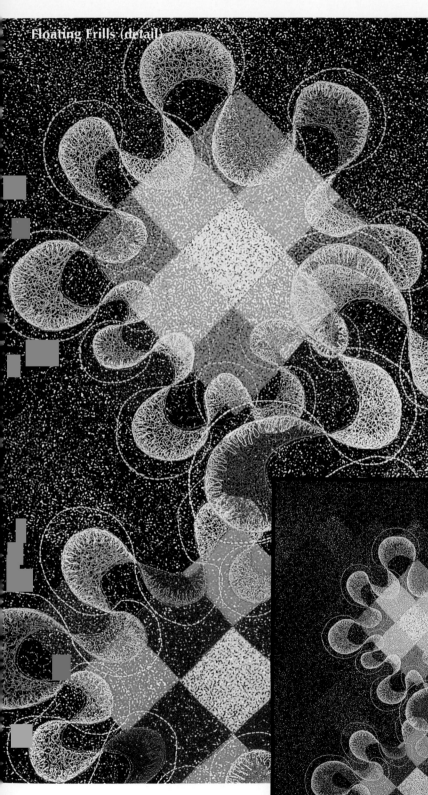

Floating Frills (detail)

TIP

Variegated threads are a little harder to use than single-color threads. If you highlight with a variegated thread, be sure the lightest color is along the edge. You need to watch the thread color as you sew. When the thread is dark, stitch toward the inside of the ribbon. When it gets lighter, move quickly back to the edge.

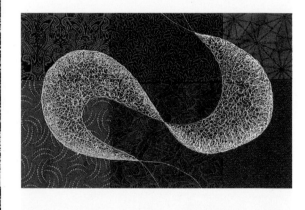

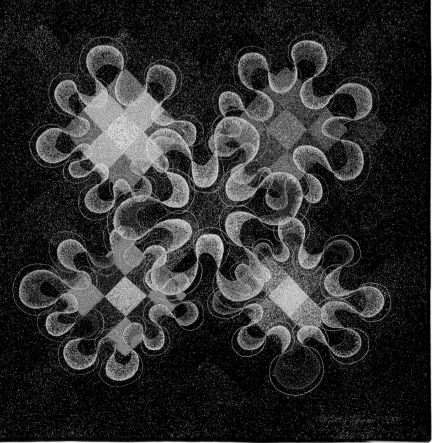

Floating Frills

by Libby Lehman, 1997, Houston, Texas, 31" x 31". Collection of Gloria Peterson.

Diamond Drift

by Libby Lehman, 1996,
Houston, Texas, 31" x 31".
Collection of Philip W.
and Christine M. Hause.

Diamond Drift (detail)

SHEER STITCHING

After you have sewn ribbons on everything in sight, you may begin to wonder, "Is this all there is?" No, ribbons are just the beginning. You can use the same technique to do any number of designs. As you can see from the photos in this book, I have used sheer stitching to make zigzags, triangles, squares, and weird shapes. You are limited only by your imagination.

SUPPLIES: Quilt top; freezer paper or iron-on tearaway stabilizer; scissors; pencil; iron and ironing board; 8" or 10" machine-embroidery hoop; fine bobbin or lingerie thread; 40-weight rayon thread (two shades, one lighter and one darker, of each color you want to use).

Transferring the Design

You can draw your design on freezer paper as described in "Drawing the Ribbon" on pages 31–32. However, when I'm trying new shapes, I cut them out of freezer paper and move them around on the quilt top until I get a pleasing design. An odd number of shapes usually works better than an even number,

and a variety of sizes add interest. Once you get a design you like, iron the freezer-paper shapes onto the top. I do this directly on my work wall.

Stitch around the shapes. If your shapes have straight lines, there is no reason to do free-motion stitching. Put the feed dogs up and sew with a straight stitch. Pivot at the corners with the needle down. Use the shapes as a guide rather than worrying about sewing exactly along the edge. If your design has a lot of curves, follow the machine setup described below and use free-motion stitching. After stitching, remove the freezer paper.

	MACHINE SETUP FOR STRAIGHT STITCHING	MACHINE SETUP FOR FREE-MOTION STITCHING
Presser foot:	Straight sewing	Darning (open or closed)
Needle: (choose one)	#80/12, #90/14 Topstitch, #75/11 Embroidery	Same
Needle position:	Down	Same
Top thread:	40-weight rayon	Same
Bobbin thread:	Bobbin/Lingerie	Same
Top tension:	Normal or slightly looser	Loose
Feed dogs:	Up	Down (or covered)
Stitch selection:	Straight	Straight or zigzag
Stitch length:	Normal (2½)	N/A
Stitch width:	0	0

Stitching the Design

Choose a thread color based on the color of your fabric. If you are sewing your design on a dark background, use a darker shade for the first filler stitches and a lighter color for highlighting. If your fabric is a light color, use lighter thread for the filler stitches and darker thread for highlighting.

1. With the marked quilt top in the hoop, place the hoop under the needle and lower the presser-foot bar. Bring the bobbin thread up. Take a few anchoring stitches and clip the thread ends. Using a straight or a zigzag stitch, fill in the shape with evenly spaced stitches; try to avoid creating a distinct pattern. Hold the hoop loosely and move it in all directions. When done, take a few anchoring stitches and clip the threads.

Shape filled in with rayon thread

Filling in with zigzag stitching

2. Load the second thread and highlight along one edge of your shape using a straight or zigzag stitch. On a dark background, use a light thread; on a light background, use a dark thread. If you do it wrong (light highlights on a light background or dark on dark), the highlight stitches may blend and disappear into the background. When done, take a few anchoring stitches and clip the threads.

Which edge you stitch along is up to you. Large shapes may require highlighting along both edges. Keep this stitching fairly close to the edge. If you stitch too heavily, you lose the effect.

Highlighting inner edge

Outer edges highlighted

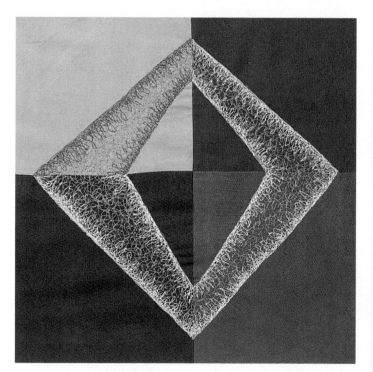

Both edges highlighted

Reverberation (detail)

Reverberation

by Libby Lehman, 1993,
Houston, Texas, 50" x 60".
Collection of Fairfield Processing
Corporation.
*Sheer-stitched zigzag shapes and
reverse-appliquéd and embroidered
stars.*

Scatter Shot

by Libby Lehman, 1996,
Houston, Texas, 55" x 55".
*Sheer-stitched squares, satin
stitching, and bobbin drawing.*

Trip Around the World: Fissures (detail)

APPLIQUÉ

*M*achine appliqué offers unlimited possibilities for quilt design. You can be as precise or as spontaneous as you want. Machine appliqué is more flexible than piecing, since you can always make changes. When I first began to make quilts, I drew everything on graph paper, colored it all in with colored pencils, then tried to translate it to fabric. This was a frustrating way to work. I found that all the fun was in the design stage, and when I moved to fabric, it became boring. I was a human copy machine. Now I work directly with fabric and trust that things will turn out. The amazing thing is, they usually do!

Trip Around the World: Fissures

by Libby Lehman, 1991,
Houston, Texas, 35" x 35".
Collection of Norma Wlos.

Direct Appliqué

The simplest way to appliqué is to cut out fabric shapes, adhere them to the quilt top, and then stitch them in place using a straight stitch. I use this method with shapes that do not overlap.

1. Piece a top layer, then cut it into segments.

2. Use a fabric gluestick or repositionable-adhesive spray to adhere the segments to a background.

3. Stitch along the edges of each piece with a narrow zigzag or a straight stitch.

4. Finish the raw edges with some decorative stitching. Refer to "Embroidery" on pages 56–72.

5. If desired, cut away the background fabric under the appliqués to reduce bulk.

Aftershocks

by Libby Lehman, 1993,
Houston, Texas, 50" x 35".
Composed of a pieced top layer that was chopped up and spread across a pieced background.

Aftershocks (detail)

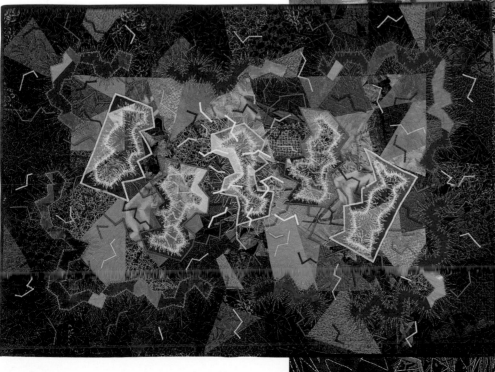

Fusible Appliqué

What a time-saver fusible web is! If you have never used it, you are in for a treat. The most convenient form is paper-backed fusible web (sold under such names as Wonder-Under, Heat-N-Bond, and Steam-A-Seam). Here are some hints that may make it easier to use:

- Read the directions. It always amazes my husband that I do this; he prefers to plunge right in, full steam ahead. And the problem with fusible web is just that—steam. Some fusibles need it, some don't. Not to mention that pressing times can vary from ten to forty-five seconds. If you heat fusible web too much or too little, it may not bond at all. Read the manufacturer's directions and pay attention!

- Look for a web that has an even coating and does not separate easily from the paper backing.

- Pick a fusible web that is appropriate for your fabric. Fusibles come in a variety of weights. A fusible that is too heavy may show on the front, and one that is too light may not bond.

- Learn how to remove the paper backing. There are two easy ways to do it. Bend a corner of the paper back on itself and let go. It should separate immediately from the fusible web.

If the paper doesn't come free, take a pin and score a line all the way across it, then pull the paper off just as you would the backing on an adhesive nametag.

The main problem I have with fusibles is that I always get the design backward. In theory, you draw the mirror image of your design on the paper, iron the fusible web onto the wrong side of the fabric, remove the paper backing, and then iron the fusible web onto your quilt. Somehow I always manage to get one too many reverses, and I end up with the mirror image on the quilt. Here's the way I get around it.

SUPPLIES: Paper-backed fusible web, pencil, straight pins, freezer paper, iron and ironing board, scissors.

1. Draw your design on freezer paper with a pencil. In the sample shown below, I have cut out the design and ironed it to the quilt top. If your design has multiple pieces, number them.

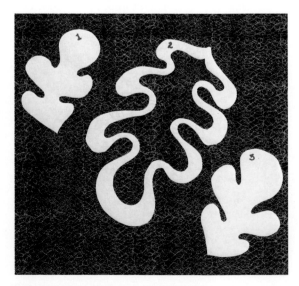

2. Place a pin or two on the quilt top to mark each pattern's position. Remove first freezer paper pattern. Iron pattern onto the right side of your chosen fabric. This method allows you to see exactly what part of the fabric will become the shape.

4. Double check to make sure the fusible is completely under the entire shape. If not, reposition the pattern. (Guess how I learned that!) Cut out the piece around the pattern with sharp scissors. With this method, the fusible is flush with the edges of the piece.

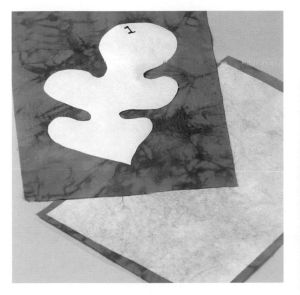

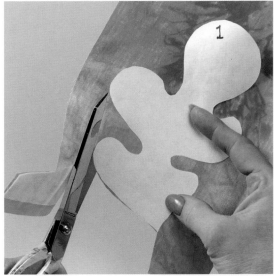

3. Cut a piece of fusible web a little bigger than the shape. Iron the fusible to the wrong side of the fabric, following the manufacturer's directions.

5. Remove the paper backing and iron the shapes in place, following the manufacturer's directions. If you aren't sure about the placement of a piece, just tap it in place with the tip of the iron to hold it temporarily. Finish fusing when you are certain of the design.

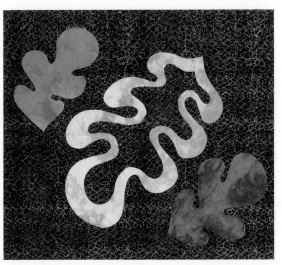

6. Refer to "Embroidery" on pages 56–72 for creative ways to finish the raw edges.

Manufacturers of fusible web brag that the bond is permanent. Don't believe them. I suppose if you are making a decorative wall piece that will never be washed and is not meant to last through the ages you won't have a problem. For any other project, however, you need to stitch around the edges of each fused piece. Use monofilament thread if you don't want the stitches to show.

I used fusible-appliqué techniques for the quilts shown on this and the following page.

Margaritaville

by Libby Lehman,
1989, Houston, Texas, 43" x 46".

Snookeroo

by Libby Lehman,
1994, Houston, Texas, 57" x 40".
This is a stylized interpretation of an original fishing fly tied by my son, Les.

Frenzy

by Libby Lehman,
1990, Houston, Texas, 76" x 86".

Sky Ribbon

by Libby Lehman, 1993, Houston, Texas,
24" x 30". Collection of Lari Ehni.

Potluck Appliqué

Potluck appliqué, a form of reverse machine appliqué, is a fun and rewarding way to work. I combine two layers of fabric, stitch through them, then cut away the top layer and see what happens. I call it "potluck" because I never know what will appear when I finish cutting. Because I don't plan too much, the work stays exciting. Give it a try.

SUPPLIES: Freezer paper, pencil, permanent marker, at least two fabric layers (pieced or whole cloth), cotton sewing thread, decorative threads, appliqué or sharp-pointed scissors.

TWO-LAYER APPLIQUÉ

Start with two layers of fabric of the same size. These can be pieced or whole cloth; the choice is yours. For best results, there should be some contrast between them. Layer both tops with right sides up. Here is a general guideline for placement:

- If both layers are whole cloth, put the lighter color on the bottom.
- If both layers are pieced, put the one with the fewest seams or the lightest colors on the bottom.
- If one layer is pieced and one layer is whole cloth, put the whole cloth on the bottom.

Following these guidelines will eliminate extra seam allowances and colors that show through the top. Baste the two layers together if the pieces are large; pin if they are small. To make it clearer, let's call the top *Layer T* and the bottom *Layer B.*

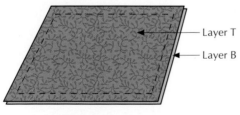

Baste or pin.

DRAWING THE DESIGN

Anytime you draw a shape for reverse appliqué, make sure it is a shape and not just a line. The top layer must "contain" the bottom layer. You cannot reverse appliqué a line. If you are unsure about your design, take a pencil and color inside the lines. If the entire page is colored in, draw again.

Lines   Shapes
                    (contain volume)

Method 1—Freezer Paper: Cut a piece of freezer paper or iron-on tearaway stabilizer the same size as the basted layers. Draw or trace the design you wish to appliqué onto the uncoated side of the paper. Iron the paper, shiny side down, on top of the basted layers. Stitch from the right side of Layer T, with the freezer paper on top.

Method 2—Direct Drawing: Turn the basted layers over and draw your design on the wrong side of Layer B with a pencil or other nonpermanent marker. Stitch from the wrong side of Layer B.

Method 3—Following the Fabric: If your fabric is printed with a design you like, use it as your pattern. If the printed design is on the top layer (Layer T), stitch from the top. If the printed design is on the bottom layer (Layer B), stitch from the back, on the wrong side of the fabric. My example had a terrific lily printed on Layer B.

Method 4—Impromptu: If you are the free-spirited type, don't draw any design. Create one as you stitch. You can stitch from either the top of Layer T or the back of Layer B.

STITCHING THE DESIGN

Decide whether you want to do straight or free-motion stitching. Regular straight stitching is great for straight lines, and free-motion stitching is best for designs with a lot of curves.

	MACHINE SETUP FOR STRAIGHT STITCHING	MACHINE SETUP FOR FREE-MOTION STITCHING
Presser foot:	Straight sewing	Darning (open or closed)
Needle: (choose one)	70/10 or 80/12 Jeans/Denim or Microtex, 75/11 Embroidery	Same
Needle position:	Down	Same
Top thread:	Cotton sewing, in color that matches top layer	Same
Bobbin thread:	Same as top thread	Same
Top tension:	Normal	Loose
Feed dogs:	Up	Down (or covered)
Stitch selection:	Straight	Straight
Stitch length:	Short (1 to ½)	N/A
Stitch width:	0	0

The design in the following example was drawn on freezer paper (Method 1).

1. Using very small stitches, stitch along all the lines of your design.

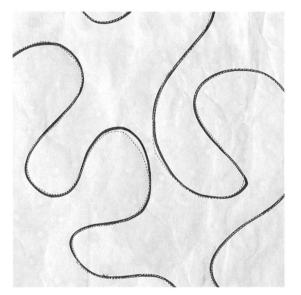

2. If you used freezer paper, tear away any paper that covers an area you will cut away. Keep the paper on any area that will remain part of the top layer. This is especially important if your design is complicated. It will help you keep track of where to cut. If you didn't use freezer paper and your design is complicated, mark the areas to be cut away with a pin, pencil, or disappearing marker.

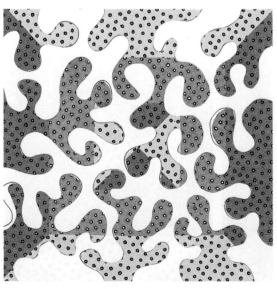

Dotted fabrics will be cut away.

3. Remove the basting.

4. Before you begin cutting, choose an area that will be Layer B. Pull the two layers apart and make a small snip in Layer T with sharp-pointed scissors. Cut away Layer T as close as possible to the stitching. This will be easier if you use appliqué scissors or embroidery scissors that cut horizontally.

By cutting horizontally, you decrease your chances of cutting through Layer B or your stitching. Besides, you never knew what to do with those scissors, so they're the sharpest ones you own!

5. Continue cutting until all your design is done. Do not cut away any of Layer B.

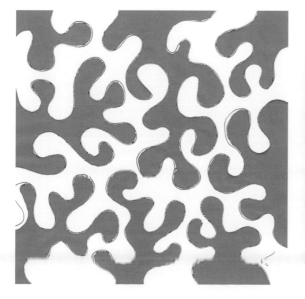

6. Remove the remaining freezer paper.

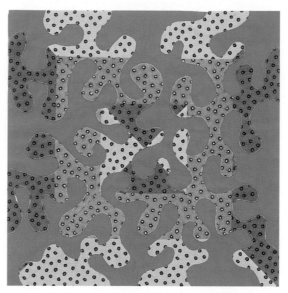

7. Refer to "Embroidery" on pages 56–72 for creative ways to finish the raw edges.

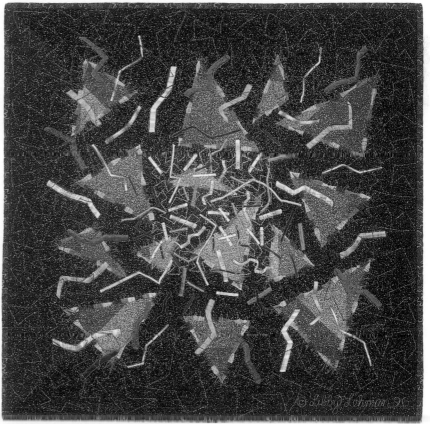

Underbrush

by Libby Lehman, 1996, Houston, Texas, 24" x 24". Collection of Valerie Sugar. *Two-layer appliqué triangles.*

Accolades

by Libby Lehman, 1993, Houston, Texas,
47" x 47". Collection of Penny Nii.
The large triangles were made with two-
layer appliqué techniques, then the small
triangles were stitched on top.

Calypso I

by Libby Lehman, 1992, Houston, Texas,
51" x 56". Collection of Reg and June Ohlson.
Two-layer appliqué flowers.

MULTI-LAYER APPLIQUÉ

Sometimes you want more than two layers of appliqué, especially for shapes that overlap. I find it much easier to begin with two layers, as described in "Potluck Appliqué" on pages 48–51, and then add other layers one at a time. The key to multi-layer appliqué is to work only two layers at a time.

1. Following the directions for two-layer appliqué, make your first shape.

2. Place a third layer under the piece you just stitched, right side up. Pin or baste the layer in place.

3. Stitch another shape using one of the methods described on page 49.

4. Pulling the layers apart, make a small slit in the piece to be cut out. Place scissors so that the bottom blade rests on top of Layer 3. Cut out the shape close to the stitching. You will be cutting through one layer in some places and through two layers in others.

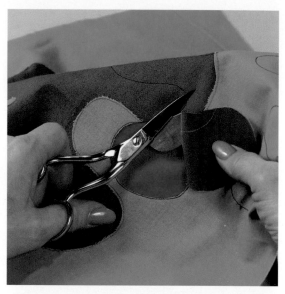

5. Repeat steps 1–4 until all the shapes have been appliquéd.

6. Refer to "Embroidery" on pages 56–72 for creative ways to finish the raw edges.

Flotsam

by Libby Lehman, 1995,
Houston, Texas, 76" x 96".
There are four appliqué layers in this quilt.

EMBROIDERY

*N*ow comes the really fun part. If you used any of my appliqué techniques, you probably noticed that you have raw edges along each seam. Some quilt artists leave these, but that makes me nervous. I think that sooner or later, the edges are going to ravel. Get out your decorative threads and browse through the following sections to choose a finishing technique.

Impact!

by Libby Lehman, 1992,
Houston, Texas, 71" x 81".

Satin Stitching

For a defined edge, nothing beats satin stitching. Satin stitching is the term used for a close zigzag stitch with a very short stitch length. It completely covers a raw edge. I have satin stitched with a narrow stitch width (*Outback Rain* on page 92), with a wide stitch width (*Flotsam* on page 55), and with varying stitch widths (*Underbrush* on page 51).

For successful satin stitching, you must stabilize the fabric. If you don't, you get an unwanted puckering effect called *tunneling*.

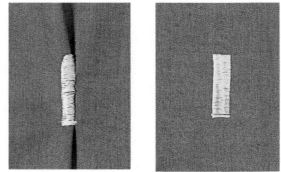

Tunneling (left), with stabilizer (right)

You can use a liquid stabilizer, an embroidery hoop, or paper. I like liquid stabilizer because it stiffens the fabric and temporarily glues the weave in place. However, liquid stabilizer does not work well if you are doing dense stitching. When your stitches are very close, the needle perforates the fabric just as though it were paper. You end up with a row of detached satin stitching.

A machine-embroidery hoop works well if your entire stitching area fits inside it. If it doesn't, the tension will be uneven when you try to tighten the hoop over the satin stitching. The best overall stabilizer for satin stitching is paper or some other tearaway.

MACHINE SETUP FOR STRAIGHT STITCHING	
Presser foot:	Embroidery
Needle: (choose one)	90/14 Topstitch, or 75/11 or 90/14 Embroidery
Needle position:	Down
Top thread:	Metallic, 40-weight rayon, or cotton embroidery
Bobbin thread:	Bobbin/lingerie or same as top thread
Top tension:	Loose
Feed dogs:	Up
Stitch selection:	Zigzag
Stitch length:	Short (1 to ½)
Stitch width:	Sewer's choice

I always start stitching on a straight area, unless I am going to vary the stitch width. In that case, I begin stitching at a point or corner, using the narrowest stitch width. To begin stitching, bring the bobbin thread to the top. If your machine has a "securing stitch," use it and clip the thread ends. Otherwise, start by taking a few straight stitches in reverse. Clip the thread ends and sew forward with a satin stitch.

There are three problem areas in satin stitching: points (angles less than 90°), corners (90° angles), and sharp curves.

POINTS AND CORNERS

There are several ways to stitch points. When I'm using a narrow zigzag stitch, my approach is to butt the ends. Just stitch to the end of one side and lift the presser foot with the needle down. If the needle is not in the right spot to stitch down the next side, lift the presser foot and shift the fabric until the next side is in line. Lower the presser foot and continue stitching.

Satin-stitched points with butted ends

If you are using a wide stitch, tapering is the answer. As you approach the point, slowly decrease the stitch width until it is narrow at the point. The stitch width will decrease evenly on both sides. Do not go down to 0, since you need to cover the exposed seam. Lift the presser foot with the needle down. Pivot the fabric, lower the presser foot, and increase the stitch width at the same pace you decreased it on the first side.

The third alternative is to miter the corners. Mitered corners look terrific but take some practice. To miter successfully, your machine must have one of the following features: 1) a variable needle position for the zigzag stitch, 2) a zigzag stitch that begins with the needle in the far left or far right position, or 3) a decorative right-angle triangle stitch. If your machine does not have one of these features, you are better off butting the ends as described previously.

Method 1: Variable Needle Positions (most Berninas)

1. Satin stitch past the corner, stopping half the distance of your stitch width from the corner. Lift the presser foot with the needle down and pivot 90°.

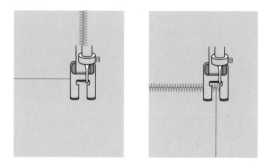

2. Look at the position of the needle in relation to the opening in the presser foot. Change the needle to the same position. For example, if the needle is to the far right, change the needle position to the far right. Make a note of the stitch width, then reduce it to 0. The needle will now be in its new position.

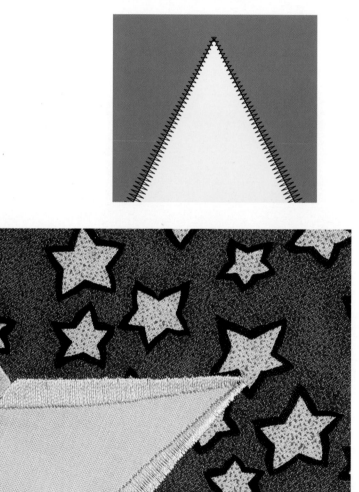

Satin-stitched points with tapered ends

3. Here comes the tricky part. As you stitch, increase the stitch width so that you are back at your original width when you come to the edge of your first row of stitching.

Since this mitered side is stitched over the first row, gaps are eliminated. Mitered stitches take practice, but the results are well worth the effort.

4. Continue to stitch without changing the needle position. Change it only when you come to another corner that goes in the opposite direction.

Method 2: Left or Right Zigzag Stitch (most Pfaffs)

Set your machine for a left or right zigzag stitch (it will probably be stitch 11 or 32). Satin stitch, following the directions for Method 1. Use the mirror-image function to switch from left to right, or vice versa.

Method 3: Triangle Stitch (some New Homes and Viking 1100, #1 or 1+)

If your machine offers a decorative stitch that is a right-angle triangle, you can use it to create mitered corners. Begin by sewing a sample triangle stitch. You may have to adjust the width or length of the satin stitch to match the desired triangle.

Satin stitch past the corner, stopping half the distance of your stitch width from the corner. Leave the needle down. For a right-turn corner, leave the needle in the right side, then pivot and stitch the triangle. Return to satin stitching. For a left pivot, use the mirror-image button.

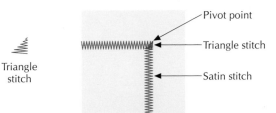

Crossfire (detail)

Crossfire

by Libby Lehman, 1996,
Houston, Texas, 46" x 46".
Mitered corners on satin-stitched squares.

CURVES

Wide curves are not hard to stitch. Simply turn the fabric gently as you stitch. It is a different story, however, if the curve is narrow. Pay attention and plan ahead.

1. Ease into the curve as soon as you approach it. You will need to pivot at several points along the curve. To pivot, stop on the outside edge of the curve with the needle down. Lift the presser foot and pivot just a little.

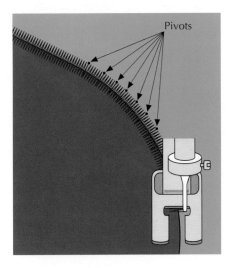

2. Make a few more stitches and pivot again. The narrower the curve, the more pivots you need to make to get a smooth line of stitching. It is much better to have too many pivots than not enough. If you stop on the inside edge when you pivot, you will get a gap.

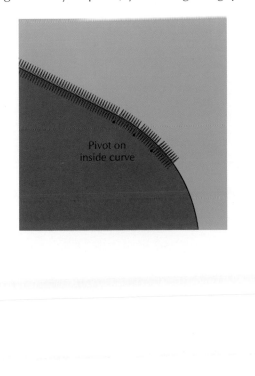

Tidewaters

by Libby Lehman, 1994, Houston, Texas, 64" x 80".

Tidewaters (detail)

Moving Target

by Libby Lehman,
1994, Houston, Texas,
55" x 27". Collection
of Catherine Anthony.
Satin-stitched circles.

Moving Target (detail)

DOUBLE NEEDLES

You can get wonderful effects by using a double needle. If your machine has a double-needle limitation button, be sure to engage it. If you do not have one, check to make sure the needles clear the presser foot before you begin stitching. The two needles have to be close together to produce a blending effect—a 1.6mm/80 or 2.0mm/80 needle works best. Use two shades of the same color for a dimensional look.

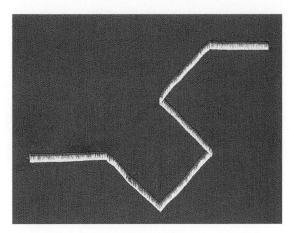

Double-needle satin stitch

Free Fall

Libby Lehman, 1994,
Houston, Texas,
41" x 41".
Private collection.

PROGRAMMED DECORATIVE STITCHES

You probably paid a lot of money for a fancy machine and haven't used more than a handful of its stitches. Now is the time to take the plunge. Get out that owner's manual and explore your machine's capabilities. Even if you don't have a lot of decorative stitches, you can do wonderful things with utility stitches. Be prudent, however, in your stitch selection. Some designs are hard to maneuver around a curved edge.

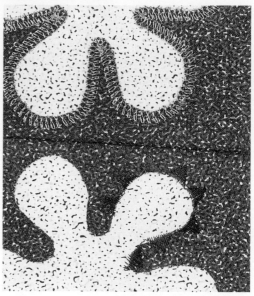

The photo shows two examples of stitching around a curve. As you can see, the decorative stitch in the upper example works well, while the triangles in the lower example do not. Always make a sample before you stitch on your quilt.

Thread Painting

You may not be an artist, but anyone can be a thread painter. Just think of the needle as a brush. Whether you stitch a realistic design or an abstract shape, painting with thread and a sewing machine gives glorious results. Using a fast foot-pedal speed and moving your hands slowly are the keys to free-motion stitching.

MACHINE SETUP FOR FREE-MOTION STITCHING	
Presser foot:	Darning (open or closed)
Needle: (choose one)	70/10 or 80/12 Jeans/Denim or Microtex, or 75/11 Embroidery
Needle position:	Down
Top thread:	Metallic, cotton or rayon embroidery
Bobbin thread:	Bobbin/lingerie
Top tension:	Loose
Feed dogs:	Down (or covered)
Stitch selection:	Straight or zigzag
Stitch length:	N/A
Stitch width:	Sewer's choice

I love the look of multiple layers of thread. My rule of thumb is to start with the darkest color and to include contrasting colors. Most of the time I do no planning. I just start with one color and keep stitching until it looks right. If I don't like a color, I pick another thread and stitch over it. Keep stitching until you are satisfied.

Try the following example.

1. Using whatever method you prefer, appliqué a flower shape to a background square.

2. Position the flower center under the needle and lower the presser foot bar. Bring the bobbin thread to the top, take a few anchoring stitches, and clip the thread tails. Using a straight stitch, sew along the center of each petal, branching out as you go. You can make as many passes on each petal as you want.

If you want the stitches to look erratic, try using a zigzag stitch in free-motion mode. You will probably have to loosen the tension more than for free-motion straight stitching, since zigzag stitching creates more drag on the thread.

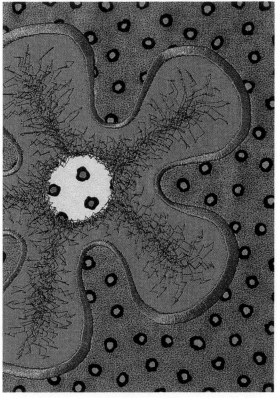

Free-motion zigzag stitch

Free-motion straight stitch

TIP

I never draw a pencil line ahead of time, on the theory that if you don't have a line to follow, you can't make a mistake. The trick is to look slightly ahead of where you are stitching rather than right at it. Breathe, keep your shoulders loose, and relax. This is fun, remember?

WRITING

One of the best ways to practice thread painting is to write your name in thread. You write your name more than anything else, so it is very familiar.

1. Stabilize the fabric and mark a line if you need a stitching guide. Just for the fun of it, try a curved line.

2. Bring the bobbin thread to the top, take a few anchoring stitches, and clip the thread tails. Write your name. My name includes the letter *i*, which I do not dot. If you must have a dot, hand sew one, using a French knot. For the letter *t*, make the cross as shown.

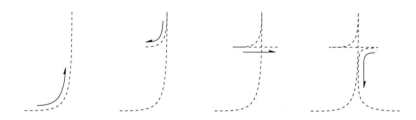

Bobbin Drawing

Sometimes you will want to play with a thread that is too thick to go through the needle eye. If it is not too thick and does not have a bumpy surface, you can use it in the bobbin and stitch from the reverse side of the quilt top. Some threads that work well for bobbin drawing are Glamour and Decor by Madeira, Candlelight and Designer 6 by YLI, and pearl cotton size 8. A good source for these threads

is your sewing machine dealer. Yarn and needlepoint shops also carry unusual threads. Look for ones that are not cut into lengths for hand sewing.

1. Wind the thread onto a bobbin, by hand or on the machine. A lot of thick threads are sold in skeins or on cards and must be wound onto an empty spool or into a ball before being wound on the bobbin.

2. Place the wound bobbin in the bobbin case. The first thing you will notice is that the bobbin tension is too tight. This makes sense since the decorative thread is much thicker than regular sewing thread.

3. You need to loosen the bobbin tension. Don't panic—you can do this! If your bobbin case is removable, take it out and look at it. There is a large screw attached to the tension spring. Remember the position of this screw so you can reset it. Adjust the screw inside a plastic bag to prevent losing it—these screws are tiny. Turn the screw to the left to loosen (lefty loosey, righty tighty). You should not have to make more than two complete turns to get the proper tension. If your bobbin case is built into the machine, consult your manual or dealer for instructions on loosening the bobbin tension. On some machines you can bypass the bobbin tension by drawing the bobbin thread through the opening at the top of the bobbin case. Since there is no tenson on the bobbin thread, it tends to make loops.

Left to loosen   Right to tighten

Bobbin Tension Adjustment

TIP

It is a good idea to get an extra bobbin case. You can leave one case adjusted for sewing-weight threads and adjust the other as needed for thick threads. Be sure to mark the extra case so you know which is which.

PROGRAMMED STITCHES

MACHINE SETUP FOR STRAIGHT STITCHING	
Presser foot:	Embroidery
Needle:	75/11 Embroidery
Needle position:	Down
Top thread:	Monofilament or thread that matches color of bobbin thread
Bobbin thread:	Decorative
Top tension:	Tighter than normal
Feed dogs:	Up
Stitch selection:	Any open decorative stitch
Stitch length:	Default or longer
Stitch width:	Default

Bobbin drawing with programmed stitches is similar to regular stitching.

1. Place the fabric, right side down, under the threaded needle. Hold on to the top thread and pull to bring the bobbin thread through the fabric. If the thread won't pop through, leave a 4" tail of bobbin thread under the fabric.

TIP

If the bobbin thread comes up as a loop, tug on the side closest to you. This is usually the tail.

---

2. Hold both threads taut and begin to stitch— if the bobbin thread is loose, it can get caught in the stitching. Do not anchor your stitching; you will tie off the threads later. Make sure that the top tension is tighter than usual so that the bobbin thread will be brought up. Occasionally, you may want the top thread to show. In that case, use regular tension.

3. When you have finished stitching, raise the presser foot and clip both threads, leaving 4" tails. Pull the bobbin thread to the top.

4. Turn the fabric over and check the stitching. Thread any bobbin-thread tails through a large-eye hand needle, then bring the thread to the back of the fabric. I like to use a needle threader. If the thread tail is short, put the needle in the fabric about halfway down, then thread it with a needle threader. Knot the top and bobbin threads. See the Tip on page 68.

TIP

Two knots that work well are the surgeon's knot and the tailor's knot.

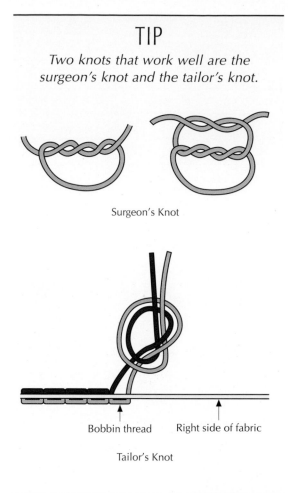

Surgeon's Knot

Bobbin thread   Right side of fabric

Tailor's Knot

Play around to see which stitches produce the best results. Remember that you are using a thick thread. Dense or detailed designs tend to look like blobs. You can control the stitch detail somewhat with your stitch-adjustment features. Don't overlook utility stitches. They look great in thick, shiny threads.

Programmed bobbin stitching

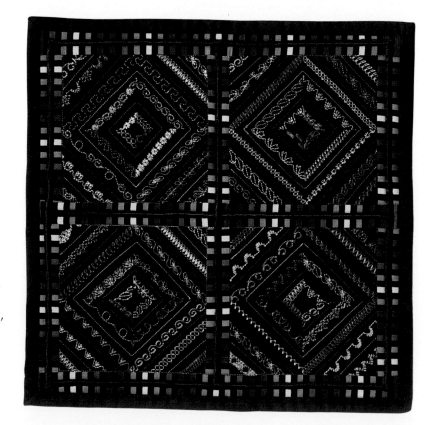

Bobbin-Drawn Sampler

by Libby Lehman, 1996, Houston, Texas, 16" x 16". *Sampler made on the Bernina 1630 using programmed stitches.*

FREE-MOTION BOBBIN DRAWING

MACHINE SETUP FOR FREE-MOTION STITCHING	
Presser foot:	Darning (open or closed)
Needle:	75/11 Embroidery
Needle position:	Down
Top thread:	Monofilament or thread that matches color of bobbin thread
Bobbin thread:	Decorative
Bobbin tension:	Loose
Top tension:	Tighter than normal
Feed dogs:	Down (or covered)
Stitch selection:	N/A
Stitch length:	N/A
Stitch width:	Sewer's choice

Drawing a Design on Paper

1. Draw or trace your design onto freezer paper or iron-on tearaway stabilizer and press it to the wrong side of the fabric. Remember to reverse the design, since you will be stitching from the wrong side.

2. Place the fabric, right side down, under the threaded needle at the start of your design. Hold on to the top thread with both hands and pull to bring the bobbin thread through the fabric and stabilizer. If it won't pop through, leave a 4" tail of bobbin thread under the fabric.

3. Hold the threads taut and begin to stitch. Don't backstitch or take tiny stitches to anchor the thread unless you want a knot on the front. Make uniform stitches using a fast foot-pedal speed while moving your hands slowly. Try to take medium-size stitches. Small stitches get lumpy and big stitches can pull the bobbin thread too tight.

4. Stop stitching at the end of your design, raise the presser foot, and clip the threads, leaving 4" tails. If your design is continuous rather than having a start and finish, stop a few stitches before you get to where you started. Continue stitching manually by turning the flywheel. On the last stitch, try to place the needle in the same hole made when you

started. Draw the needle up, raise the presser foot, and pull the bobbin thread up. Clip the threads, leaving 4" tails. Tie the thread tails and clip any extra thread.

Writing

You can also use free-motion bobbin drawing to write.

1. Write out whatever you want to stitch. I find it helpful to do this on graph paper to get the height and spacing even.

2. Turn the paper over and trace the writing onto freezer paper or iron-on tearaway stabilizer. Press the design onto the wrong side of the fabric. The writing will be in reverse, a mirror image.

3. Follow steps 2–4 of "Drawing a Design on Paper" on page 69.

Following a Fabric Motif

If your fabric has a terrific overblown flower or snazzy star, why not use it as your pattern for bobbin drawing? Stabilize the fabric however you prefer. If you can see the design from the wrong side of the fabric, simply turn it over and stitch, following steps 2–4 of "Drawing a Design on Paper" on page 69. If you cannot see the design through the fabric, you will need to transfer it. Do this by using a light table or by taping the fabric, wrong side toward you, to a window. Trace the design (mirror image) on the back of the fabric or onto freezer paper that has been pressed to the back of the fabric.

Stitching Spontaneously

You don't need to follow a pattern. For a very free design, stabilize the fabric, place it back-side up under the needle, and go for it!

Firebrand (detail)

Spontaneous bobbin drawing done with decorative yellow thread

Quilting

Bobbin drawing creates a wonderful defined quilting line. The only drawback is that you can't see the front of your quilt for design purposes. I solve this problem by first quilting the major lines or shapes from the front of the quilt using monofilament thread, then turning it over and bobbin drawing from the back. I like to use a solid color or a very small-scale print for the quilt back since this makes it easier to see where I am stitching.

You can bobbin quilt using either the programmed-stitch or free-motion methods described previously. Finish by threading the tied thread tails through a large-eye needle. Pull the needle through the top layer into the batting for about 2" to 3", then back out. Clip the tails. If the threads are very thick, tie each one off and pull them through separately.

Couching

Some decorative threads or trims are too thick or uneven to go through the needle eye or the bobbin. These threads include yarn, braid, cord, rickrack, lace, and most ribbons. They must be couched; that is, they must be laid on the fabric and stitched in place.

The hardest part of couching is figuring out what to do with the ends. My advice is to try to plan your trim placement so that the ends are either encased in the seam allowances or covered by other decorative elements. If you must end the trims in an open area, thread the tails through a large-eye hand needle and pull them to the back. If the trim is too large for this, try clipping the ends and applying a drop of fray preventative.

Accolades (detail)

Chenille yarn couched on the quilt surface

Flat trims, such as rickrack, decorative braid, and ribbon, can be easily couched. Place them on a stabilized fabric and stitch. There are special feet available to hold the trim in place while you stitch. Use monofilament thread and a straight or very narrow zigzag stitch if you don't want the stitching to show. Use decorative threads and stitches for an accent.

TIP

You may want to position your trims before stitching, especially if the design is intricate. I use a fabric gluestick, fusible web, or spray adhesive for the job.

If you're using a narrow trim, such as ¼"-wide ribbon, look for a double needle as close as possible to the same width, and straight stitch in place.

TIP

Always couch satin ribbon. Never attach it by straight stitching down one side, across the end, then back up the other. The stitches pull on one side more than the other, creating a wavy look. While we're on the subject of satin ribbon, be sure to use a new needle. One tiny burr can ruin the entire ribbon. I know, because I've done it!

The wider the trim, the less it will bend or curve. If you want to do a very curvy pattern, you'll be happier with a narrow trim. Also, look for trims that are cut on the bias.

Round trims are easiest to attach with a cording or piping foot. The bottoms of these feet have a rounded groove where the trim can ride. The cording, or braiding, foot has a hole in the front through which you can thread the trim to guide it under the needle. I find it easiest to thread the trim through the hole before I attach the foot to the machine.

There are also separate guides available that attach to the front of your machine. They are pieces of plastic with small holes punched at regular intervals and a suction cup on one side. Position the suction cup on your machine just above the needle, thread the trims through the holes, and stitch over them.

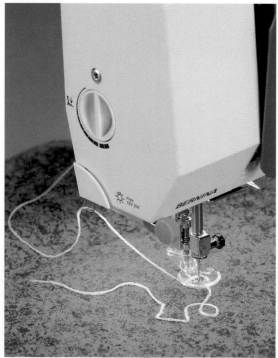

Finishing

La Vie Dansante (detail)

BACKING

There are as many opinions on quilt backs as there are quilters. Some quilt artists like to piece a back that complements the top. Others use any scrap fabrics that are the right size. While I admire an artistically designed back, I most often use one fabric that doesn't distract from the quilt top. I consider my quilts art and would not think of going to an art gallery, turning a painting over, and looking at the back. If you see "backart" on my quilts, it means I did not have enough fabric and had to piece a back. This usually happens late at night when I can't get to the store!

When I see good backing fabric, I try to buy five to ten yards of it. There is nothing more frustrating than realizing that you don't have the right backing fabric when you are ready to quilt. What is a good backing fabric? That depends. A lot of my quilt tops have dark backgrounds. I like to back those tops with a random print that has a black background so I can use black bobbin or lingerie thread in the bobbin. If I am going to quilt with bobbin-drawing methods, I use a solid color or a muted print so I can see where to stitch.

There has been debate over how to piece the back if the top is wider than 44". Some quilters consider it much better to cut two lengths, split one of them, and sew the halves on each side of the remaining piece. Personally, I don't understand the logic behind this. It seems to me that one seam down the middle is just as good, if not better, than two on the sides. You might want to take Mary Elllen Hopkins's approach and sew diagonal seams!

Gift Wrapped

by Libby Lehman, 1997, Houston, Texas, 20" x 20".

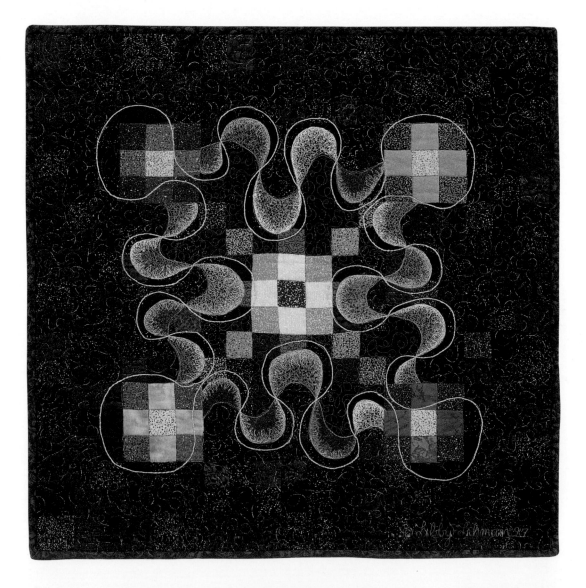

BATTING

Entire books have been devoted to batting. As with all other quilting supplies, get the best batting you can afford. Cheap batting is the worst bargain in town after cheap thread. If you are going to put all that time and effort into your quilt, you don't want it disintegrating after one washing.

Your choice of batting depends on the look you want and the function of the quilt. Let's look at several of the most popular battings.

Cotton

Cotton is the preferred choice of batting for most machine quilters. It gives a flat look that adds contours to the quilt surface without being too puffy. Most cotton batting needs to be quilted fairly closely. Some people prewash their batting, but I don't. Most of my quilts are wall pieces that probably won't get dirty or require washing. I use Fairfield's Soft Touch. Even though it is 100% cotton, you don't have to quilt every 2" as you do with other cotton battings. It also lives up to its name; it is very soft and a breeze to machine quilt. I have also used and liked Fairfield's Cotton Classic, which is 80% cotton and 20% polyester. Other good brands are Hobbs, Warm and Natural, and Mountain Mist.

Polyester

Polyester is the most readily available batting; it comes in the widest range of sizes and weights. The low lofts are very thin and lightweight. At the other end are extra, or high, lofts that work best for puffy, tied quilts. Fairfield, Hobbs, and Mountain Mist all make good polyester battings. Be sure to look for bonded battings, which have treated surfaces that help keep the synthetic fibers from bearding, that is, from migrating through the quilt top. The bonded fibers also allow you to leave more room between quilting lines. Polyester batting is slicker than cotton and tends to shift, especially with free-motion quilting. Be sure your basting is close together to prevent shifting.

Wool

I suppose wool batting would have more appeal for me if I lived in Montana or Minnesota. Houston's humid climate is not conducive to a warm wool batting. You can wash wool batting, but it tends to shrink noticeably. Most manufacturers advise dry cleaning. Wool is easy to quilt, although it is more expensive than cotton or polyester. Some art quilters like to use wool army blankets instead of batting, especially for heavy quilts. The stiffness and density of the wool blanket keeps the quilt from sagging.

Silk

Silk is your most expensive batting option. In order to prevent bearding, you need to sandwich the batting between two layers of China silk. Dry cleaning is also recommended. I have not experimented with silk batting much due to all these conditions. New products come out all the time, however, and you may be able to find a silk batting that eliminates some of these concerns.

No matter which batting you choose, let it relax before you baste. Theoretically, you can unpack batting before you go to bed or before you leave for the day, and the wrinkles will smooth out in a few hours. However, it almost never works like that for me. I undo the packaging and spread it out over the backing, then I steam it with my Euro-Pro iron or with a hand-held steamer. Steaming works especially well with cotton-polyester blends. Along with getting rid of creases and folds, steaming makes the batting surface softer.

BASTING

Congratulations! You have completed your top and are now ready to quilt it. The next step is the least favorite of most quilters, myself included—basting. I hate to tell you this, but basting the top, batting, and back together is essential for a successful quilt. There is a bright spot on the horizon, however. I am about to let you in on my method for (almost) painless basting.

One winter, my family was on a ski trip to Aspen. Mother had finished a top and was ready to baste it, but the condo we were renting had no floor or table big enough. We decided to try the wall. After taking down a large painting, we taped the backing to the wall with masking tape, right side to the wall. Next came the batting, and finally the top. Since everything was spread out evenly, we could baste in any direction rather than from the center out. The wall method also saved wear and tear on our backs and knees. It worked so well that I have been doing it ever since.

At home, I use straight pins instead of tape to pin everything into my work wall. My current work wall is made up of 2' x 4' acoustical tiles, which come painted white on one side. These are fairly inexpensive and readily available at home improvement stores. Try to find ones with as little texture as possible. Using nails or glue, attach them to your studio wall as close together as possible. I have drawn horizontal lines across the entire wall every 2" to help with alignment. Use a permanent marker to do this. I don't like to cover the tiles with anything since that allows me to stitch directly on the top while it is pinned in place. I can also use my iron on a quilt that is pinned to the wall without any damage to the tiles.

Make sure all layers are evenly spread and wrinkle-free, but do not stretch them. Stretching will lead to disaster when you remove the pins and everything shrinks back to normal.

Basting Guns

I have had good luck using a Quiltak Basting Gun. This machine is similar to the one retail stores use to attach price tags to garments, except that the needle is finer. You stick the point through all three layers of the quilt sandwich and pull the trigger. A plastic tab passes through the hollow needle, leaving a tab on both sides. If this tab is not tight enough (there is a $\frac{1}{4}$" shank), simply take a stitch with the needle before you pull the trigger. This will leave both tabs on the right side.

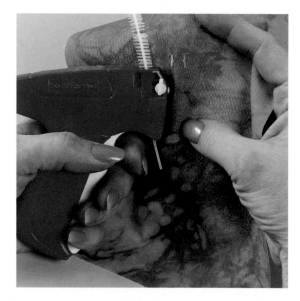

When using this machine, you must baste from the outside edges toward the center. I usually start on the left side, work across the bottom, and then move up both sides. Leave the top edge for last. This way, gravity helps to keep everything straight. Place the tabs at least every 3".

PROS: The tabs are easy to remove and will not break your needle if you accidentally sew over them.

CONS: The gun and tabs are expensive. Because of the thicker needle, it is not suitable for very tight-weave or fragile fabrics. The tabs are not reusable.

Safety-Pin Basting

My second choice for basting is with safety pins. Be sure to test the pins for sharpness before you buy them. Use size 1 safety pins, which are 1" long and are nickel plated so they won't rust. Some people find the new curved safety pins a convenience, but they are not made for us left-handers. For a 50" x 50" quilt, you will need at least three hundred pins. That's not a typo—you need tons of pins to do this right!

To pin baste, prepare the backing, batting, and quilt top as described previously. Place safety pins about 3" apart over the entire quilt top, leaving them open. This is why you need so many. If the pins are farther apart, the layers can shift. Make sure the pins go through all three layers. You can pin baste in any order, although I usually start in the upper left and work down to the lower right.

After all the pins are in place, go back and close them. If you do this as you go, it can distort the layers. I use a dowel with a screw tip to help close the pins. Place the pointed end of the pin in any of the grooves and push down on the other end until the pin closes.

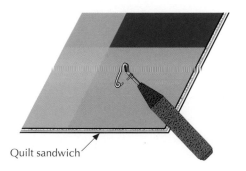

Quilt sandwich

Pros: Quicker than thread basting. Safety pins are reusable.

Cons: You must remove the pins as you stitch. The pins are hard to close unless you have a tool to help.

Thread Basting

You can do traditional thread basting on a wall. Tape or pin the layers as described previously. Thread a long or curved needle with a long length of white basting thread— silk thread is wonderful because it doesn't leave even a small hole, but it is expensive. Don't use a dark thread on light fabrics because it can leave a dark hole when removed. Insert the needle in the center of the quilt through all three layers. A spoon can help to push the layers down and get the point of the needle back to the top.

Pull the thread halfway, leaving a long tail. Take large stitches until you reach one side of the quilt top. Leave a thread tail rather than tying a knot. Go back to the center and thread the other end of your thread. Stitch to the other side. As with the other two methods, you can baste in any direction since the entire project is already pinned or taped in place.

If it is critical that part of the quilt top stay in a certain position, you can baste with a whipstitch. Take a ½"-wide stitch, move up or down about one inch, then take another stitch. This is easier with a curved needle and is time-consuming but ensures good results.

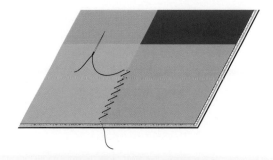

Pros: Ensures that the layers won't shift; inexpensive. Quilting over basting threads won't break your needle.

Cons: Time-consuming.

Fabric-Adhesive Sprays

My favorite method of basting is using a temporary spray adhesive, such as 505, HRFive, or Sulky Temporary Spray Adhesive. I always spray in a well ventilated area or outdoors. The last thing I need in my studio is spray glue covering everything, even if it is temporary!

To use, spray a light coat of adhesive on the wrong side of the quilt back. Pin this to your work wall with the wrong side facing out. Lay the batting on next and smooth in place. Spray the wrong side of the quilt top and then spread it on top of the batting. Take the quilt sandwich off the wall and press both sides to make sure there are no wrinkles.

Hidden Agendas

by Libby Lehman, 1994, Houston, Texas, 39" x 39". Pilgrim/Roy Collection.

MACHINE QUILTING

After you have basted your quilt sandwich together, take some time to get your sewing space set up for quilting. If you are making a small wall quilt, this will not take long. For a larger piece, you will need to make room for the project. Begin by getting rid of any potential hazards lying around. That half-cup of tea will invariably get spilled smack dab in the middle of your quilt. Next, make sure you have enough horizontal surface to support your quilt, both before you quilt it and after it passes through the machine. I sew on a large table. When I quilt, I lower the ironing board and move it to the left side of the machine.

Make sure your chair is comfortable and the correct height. I like to sit rather high so that my arms are almost at waist level. I treated myself to an ergonomic upholstered office swivel chair last year, and it has been worth its weight in gold. Finally, give the machine a thorough cleaning, oil it, and insert a brand-new needle. Your choice of needle depends on your choice of thread. See "Machine Needles" on pages 14–16.

Now comes the problem of getting all that stuff under the needle. Several expert quilters recommend folding the quilt neatly into thirds and securing the parts you are not working on with bicycle clips. I tried this and I guess it worked pretty well, but it sure was a lot of trouble. I use the "round 'em up, head 'em out" approach (maybe it's the Texan in me!). This means you gather up the quilt sandwich as best you can, throw it over your shoulder if you have to, and quilt like mad. Don't force or pull the quilt sandwich under the needle. This is asking for trouble.

Position the sandwich, quilt about 6", then move the sandwich forward so that you can easily move the portion under the needle, without pulling. Try to quilt from the center out. The worst thing you can do is to stitch around the outside first. This fences you in and allows you no leeway in preventing puckers.

A new innovation in free-motion quilting is the Bernina Stitch Regulator (BSR for short). This patented technology is available on certain Bernina models (check with your dealer). Attach the BSR foot and you have variable speed and adjustable stitch length and width (width adjustment available only on models equipped with zigzag BSR), plus you are in control. This is like magic to me!

There are two modes. When engaged, Mode 1 stitches at a low speed whether you move the fabric or not. Mode 2 only stitches when you move the fabric. I use Mode 1 for curves and Mode 2 when I want points. In either mode, there is an auto shutoff feature after 7 seconds. This is sort of like having cruise control on your sewing machine. It is a wonderful "extra", but there is still a driver involved. Regardless of the method you use, quilting is still a skill. It takes practice to produce quality.

Don't let machine quilting become a chore. Remember to relax your shoulders, sit up straight and breathe. I try to get up and move around about every 90 minutes.

Straight-Line Quilting

MACHINE SETUP FOR STRAIGHT STITCHING	
Presser foot:	Walking
Needle:	Depends on thread choice
Needle position:	Down
Top thread:	Monofilament, cotton, rayon, or metallic
Bobbin thread:	Bobbin/lingerie or cotton
Top tension:	Adjust as necessary
Feed dogs:	Up
Stitch selection:	Straight
Stitch length:	Default setting or sewer's choice
Stitch width:	0

A walking foot helps to feed the layers evenly. Some Pfaff machines have a built-in walking foot that simply snaps into place. Other companies offer a walking foot as an accessory. If the manufacturer of your machine does not offer one, look for a generic walking foot that might fit. This foot will be a godsend if you plan to do a lot of straight-line quilting.

To begin straight-line quilting, adjust the tension. When working with metallic thread, reduce the top tension to compensate for the thin bobbin thread. With other threads, you may need to tighten the top tension. Every machine and thread combination is different.

Once the tension is correct, bring the bobbin thread to the top, reduce the stitch length almost to 0, and take a few tiny stitches in place. If your machine has a securing stitch, use it instead to anchor the threads. Return the stitch length to your preferred setting and quilt. End the stitching line the same way. Quilt all the lines in the same direction to prevent puckering.

The first thing I do is to quilt any straight lines that need to stay perfectly straight. For example, it was important that the grid in *Sheer Rhapsody,* shown on page 19, remain square. I began by quilting along each vertical and horizontal seam line. Called *quilting in-the-ditch,* this line of quilting is done right next to the down side of a seam, the one without the seam allowance. I used monofilament thread because I did not want to emphasize the lines; I just wanted them to be straight. Next, I went back and added free-motion decorative quilting in 40-weight rayon thread. If I had done just the free-motion quilting, it would have pulled the pieced squares in different directions and distorted the straight seams.

TIP

Try using a single-hole throatplate to prevent puckering and skipped stitches. This plate has a small, round hole just big enough to accommodate the needle. The quilt sandwich stays flat against the bed of the machine, and you get a nice clean stitch. Just be sure to change back to the standard plate before you try to zigzag stitch, or you will break your needle.

Quilting guides are helpful for quilting parallel lines without having to mark them. They are attached to the presser foot and can be adjusted for different widths. Begin by stitching one line. Adjust the guide to the desired width, position the guide on the first line, and stitch the second line. The guide rides on the first line to keep the second line parallel. If you want to quilt lines farther apart than the guide allows, mark the lines with masking tape.

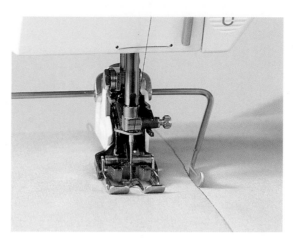

Free-Motion Quilting

MACHINE SETUP FOR FREE-MOTION STITCHING	
Presser foot:	Darning (open or closed)
Needle:	Depends on thread choice
Needle position:	Down
Top thread:	Monofilament, cotton, rayon, or metallic
Bobbin thread:	Bobbin/lingerie or cotton
Top tension:	Adjust as necessary
Feed dogs:	Down (or covered)
Stitch selection:	Straight
Stitch length:	N/A
Stitch width:	0

I much prefer free-motion quilting, even for straight lines. If you have to turn a lot of corners, you will soon appreciate the freedom of stitching without having to turn the whole quilt every time.

Use a darning or free-motion quilting foot. On the Bernina, the 29C quilting foot is a clear plastic foot with a large rectangular opening. It holds the fabric in place while the needle is down and is easy to see through. If your machine doesn't have one of these, check out the Big Foot or a spring needle.

I start by quilting around any major design elements. Position the quilt sandwich under the needle. Bring the bobbin thread up to the top. Take a few stitches in place to anchor the thread and clip the thread tails. Quilt around the design. To finish, take a few more stitches in place and clip the thread tails.

When quilting a large piece, I place the machine at a 45° angle on my table. Use the regular bed for the machine rather than an extension. This gives me more room on either side of the needle, yet I can still see the control panel. The space between the needle and the motor is the narrowest place the quilt has to pass through. It is also where your hand needs to be. This method only works when you are not using the feed dogs to guide the fabric in a straight line.

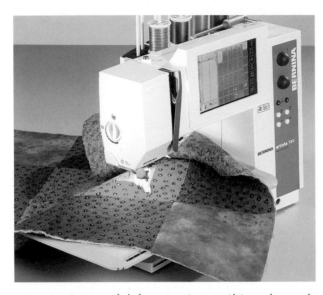

Successful free-motion quilting depends a lot on pacing. Learn to move your hands slowly and the foot pedal at a fast, even speed. To help move the quilt sandwich, I use small circles of rubber sold as Needle Grabbers. You can also cut up any kind of rubber, such as bottle top removers or even place mats. Just put these on the surface of the quilt and put your fingers on top of them. The rubber creates traction that helps your fingers get a hold on everything. Finger cots or secretarial fingertips may work for some people, but they make my fingers sweat.

Another tool new to the market is Quilt Sew Easy by Heavenly Notions. This open hoop has pieces of foam on the bottom and handles on the top. Place it around the area you are quilting and move the quilt with the handles. For large quilts, there are two hoops that mesh. This is especially helpful for quilters who have weak hands or arthritis.

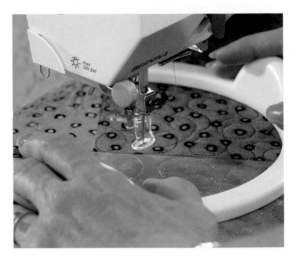

After quilting around any major design elements, I quilt the background. I have learned from experience that you need to quilt the background evenly. Your quilt will pucker if you have some areas that are heavily quilted and others that have no quilting at all. Traditionally, the best way to cover a background is to stipple quilt. With this technique, you stitch a small, circuitous pattern.

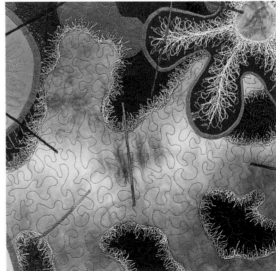

Some quilters claim that stippling stitches should never loop back or cross one another. I can't for the life of me figure out why this method has become so sacred. I cross over my stitching line all the time and have yet to be nabbed by the quilt police!

My favorite way of quilting a background is to meander, or stitch lots of small loops. It is also the fastest way I know to get the top quilted. Always work from the center out to the edges. Begin by bringing up the bobbin thread. Hold the threads taut and take a few stitches in place. Clip the thread tails. Make a small loop, being sure to cross over your first stitches to double-anchor them. Continue to make loops in both directions.

When you want to end, make a final loop, taking some small stitches at the end. Clip the thread tails. By beginning and ending with a loop, you can disguise where you started and stopped stitching.

Some designs are better suited to a geometric pattern than curves. In that case, I make triangles rather than loops. Again, start and end your stitching by making a triangle.

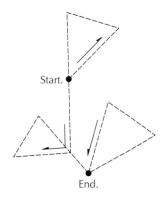

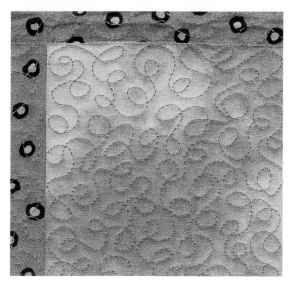

Meander quilting

You can make any size loop you want. Sometimes I vary the size to add dimension.

Geometric meandering

TYING

An alternative to quilting is tying, or holding the three layers together with decorative ties rather than quilting stitches. Tying is most often used with an extra-loft batting, which is very difficult to quilt. Tying by machine is much easier than tying by hand. You can use thread, yarn, ribbon, floss, or just about any other material that can be tied. You still need to baste or tack the layers together. Place ties according to the recommended quilting-line spacing for the batting you are using.

Ties are most often placed at the intersections of blocks but can also be placed in a random pattern. Utilitarian ties are almost invisible, while decorative ties strut their stuff.

Utilitarian Tying

MACHINE SETUP FOR STRAIGHT STITCHING	
Presser foot:	Walking or embroidery
Needle:	70/10 Microtex or Jeans/Denim
Needle position:	Up
Top thread:	Monofilament or cotton
Bobbin thread:	Bobbin/lingerie or cotton
Top tension:	Adjust
Feed dogs:	Up
Stitch selection:	Satin or zigzag
Stitch length:	Short
Stitch width:	1½ to 3

The least obvious method of tying is to use monofilament thread to tack the layers together. You can use bobbin/lingerie, monofilament, or cotton thread in the bobbin. Use a bar-tack stitch if your machine offers one. Otherwise, set your machine for satin stitching.

1. Position the quilt sandwich where you want the first tie. Lower the presser foot and bring the bobbin thread to the top. Bartack or take about 4 to 6 satin stitches. Lock the satin stitches with a securing stitch.

2. Lift the presser foot and move the quilt sandwich to the next spot for a tie. Repeat the process. There is no need to clip the threads until you are done.

3. Clip the top threads; then turn the quilt over. On the back, give the thread a tug before you clip it. This will pull the top thread to the back. Apply a dot of fray preventative on the back of each tack to reinforce it.

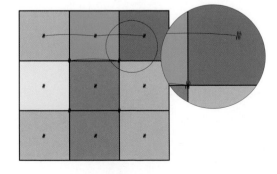

Decorative Programmed Tying

MACHINE SETUP FOR STRAIGHT STITCHING	
Presser foot:	Embroidery
Needle:	Depends on thread choice
Needle position:	Up
Top thread:	Cotton, rayon, metallic, or other decorative thread
Bobbin thread:	Bobbin/lingerie (for metallic) or same as top thread
Top tension:	Adjust as necessary
Feed dogs:	Up
Stitch selection:	Any dense, decorative pattern
Stitch length:	Default
Stitch width:	Default

This is a great chance to use those fancy stitches you paid so much to get. Choose one that has a dense, filled-in element. You may want to use different elements over the quilt to add fun and interest.

1. Program your machine to do one complete element.

2. After stitching, lift the presser foot and move to the next spot without clipping the threads. Repeat across the quilt surface.

3. When all the tacks are stitched, clip the top threads first, then turn the quilt over. On the back, give the thread a tug before you clip it. This will pull the top thread to the back. Add a dot of fray preventative if desired.

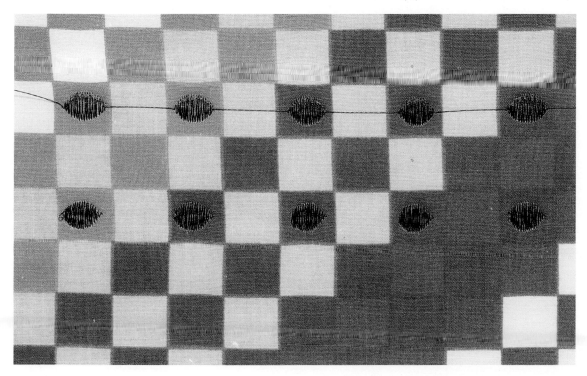

Free-Motion Tying

MACHINE SETUP FOR FREE-MOTION STITCHING	
Presser foot:	Free-motion quilting or darning
Needle:	70/10 or 80/12 Jeans/Denim
Needle position:	Up
Top thread:	Monofilament or thread that matches the ties
Bobbin thread:	Monofilament or thread that matches the quilt back
Top tension:	Adjust as necessary
Feed dogs:	Down
Stitch selection:	Straight
Stitch length:	N/A
Stitch width:	0

Free-motion tying comes closest to resembling hand tying. You can determine the length of your ties by tying a piece of string with whatever knot you want to use and then measuring the string. Cut pieces of ribbon, floss, or yarn into the desired length.

1. Place a length of your tie in the first spot. Lower the presser foot and stitch across the tie, moving the quilt slowly forward and then backward several times. This anchors the tie in place.

2. Lift the presser foot and move to the next tie location without clipping the threads and repeat.

3. When everything is anchored, clip the extra threads and tie the knots or bows.

BINDING

*T*here are many ways to finish the edges of a quilt and several good books on the subject. The one I always turn to is *Happy Endings* by Mimi Dietrich. All my art quilts are finished with a double-fold binding. The double thickness gives added stability to the edge and a nice finished look. Some designs look better with the binding turned to the back so that it does not show.

Whichever binding method I choose, I square up the top first. My sewing table is covered with a large cutting mat, which in turn is usually covered with lots of other stuff.

After clearing the decks, I square up the quilt using a large Plexiglas square and a rotary cutter. Start by squaring up one corner, then work your way around the quilt. If it is a very large quilt, I move to the floor and measure every step of the way. This is one of the most rewarding parts because when you are through trimming off the excess edges, it finally looks like a quilt!

Choosing a fabric for the binding depends a lot on the front quilt design. My personal preference is a dark binding. It acts as a period at the end of a sentence, giving closure. Sometimes I piece closely related dark fabrics together to keep the dark look while adding texture and interest.

La Vie Dansante

by Libby Lehman, 1992, Houston, Texas, 43" x 58".
Collection of Sarah Youngblood.
Finished with ½"-wide front-edge binding.

Front-Edge Binding

Strips cut on the crosswise grain have a little stretch, while strips cut lengthwise have very little. I cut binding lengthwise, with the straight of grain. Bias binding is necessary only for curved or irregularly shaped quilt edges.

	MACHINE SETUP FOR STRAIGHT STITCHING
Presser foot:	Patchwork, Little Foot, straight-stitch foot, or walking foot
Needle:	80/12 Jeans/Denim or Microtex
Needle position:	Down
Top thread:	Cotton
Bobbin thread:	Cotton
Top tension:	Normal
Feed dogs:	Up
Stitch selection:	Straight
Stitch length:	Default
Stitch width:	0

1. Figure the amount of binding by measuring all four sides of the quilt and adding 10". For example, if your quilt is 20" x 36", you will need 122" of binding (20 + 20 + 36 + 36 + 10 = 122). You can get by with as little as 4" extra, but I don't like to live dangerously.
2. Cut enough strips, either on the crosswise or lengthwise grain, to yield the required amount of binding.

For ¼" finished binding,
cut strips 2¼" wide.

For ½" finished binding,
cut strips 3¼" wide.

For ¾" finished binding,
cut strips 5¼" wide.

For 1" finished binding,
cut strips 7¼" wide.

3. Piece the strips together by stitching the ends straight across. Some experts recommend joining the ends on the bias to eliminate bulk, but I've never noticed a problem. Pressing the straight seams open must take care of it.
4. Fold the binding in half lengthwise, wrong sides together, and press. Fold under one end about ½".

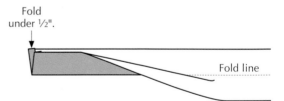

Fold under ½".

Fold line

5. Place the folded end of the binding somewhere along the upper edge of the quilt top, raw edges together, and pin it in place. Make sure the binding seam doesn't coincide with a corner. If it does, readjust the placement to avoid bulk at the corners. Begin stitching about 1" from the folded edge. Success depends on using a seam allowance the same width as the binding. If you want a ¼"-wide binding, use a ¼"-wide seam allowance.

6. As you near a corner, mark ¼" from the edge of the quilt with a pin. You can eliminate this step if you are using a presser foot with ¼" markings, such as Bernina's size 37 Patchwork or Lynn Graves' Little Foot. These feet have an indentation that lets you know when the needle is ¼" from the edge. Stitch to the pin or ¼" mark and leave the needle down. Lift the presser foot and pivot the quilt until the corner points directly at you.

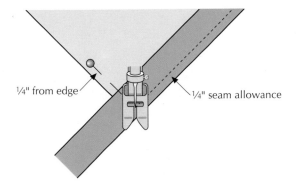

¼" from edge   ¼" seam allowance

If you are using a different width for your seam allowance and binding, stop at that point. For example, stop ½" from the edge if you want a ½" binding.

7. Remove the pin and stitch to the corner and off the quilt at a 45° angle.

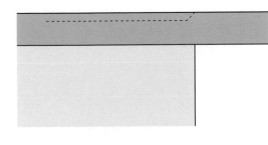

8. Move the quilt so that the next side is ready to sew. Fold the binding back along the 45°-angle seam, then down until the raw edges of the binding and the quilt are aligned. Stitch along the second side, beginning at the top of the quilt. Repeat until all the corners are stitched.

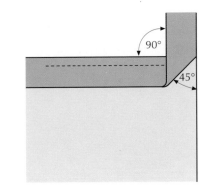

90°

45°

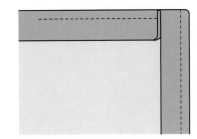

9. Stitch the last side until you are about 1½" from the folded edge. Stop with the needle down. Cut the binding so that there is a ½" overlap. Place the cut edge inside the folded edge and pin to the top. Finish stitching.

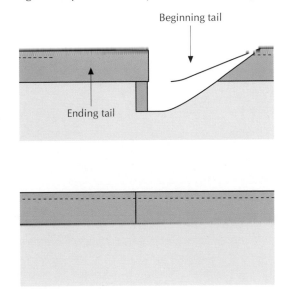

Beginning tail

Ending tail

10. Turn the binding to the back by pressing the seams toward the binding.

11. Turn the quilt over. Press the binding to the back, using a ¼"-wide strip of fusible web. The fusible web eliminates the need for pins.

12. Stitch the folded edge by hand or turn the quilt over and stitch in-the-ditch along the binding seam. Hand stitch the corner folds. This is not necessary technically since there is no way the corners will come loose. Judges, however, are pretty sticky about it. If you are entering your quilt in competition, stitch them down or suffer the consequences!

Silent Partners

by Libby Lehman, 1995, Houston, Texas, 35" x 35". Private collection.
Finished with a ¼"-wide front-edge binding.

Back-Edge Binding

I use this method when I don't want the binding to show on the front. I still use a double binding for stability. If the edges of the quilt are the same color or fabric, choose a binding to match. If not, use the same fabric as the back or one that complements it.

1. To calculate the amount of binding to cut, measure the perimeter of the quilt and add 4".
2. Cut strips 2" wide on the straight of grain (cut on the bias if your quilt edge is curved).
3. Stitch pieces together to form a continuous binding. Fold under ¼" at one end, then fold in half lengthwise and press.
4. Place the end with the fold along the top of the quilt, raw edges together. Start stitching about 1" from the folded edge with a ¼"-wide seam allowance. Stop with the needle down when you are ¼" from the corner.

5. Lift the presser foot and pivot 90°. Turn the binding until the raw edges line up with the next side. Continue stitching.

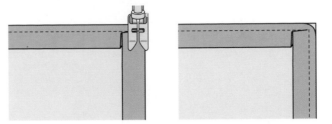

6. Repeat until all the corners are stitched. Stitch the last side until you are about 1½" from the folded edge. Stop with the needle down. Cut the binding so that there is a ½" overlap. Place the cut edge inside the folded edge and pin to the top. Finish stitching.
7. Clip the corners to get rid of excess bulk. Press the binding away from the quilt. Turn it to the back so that none of the binding shows on the front of the quilt. Press in place with a ¼"-wide strip of fusible web. Hand stitch in place or stitch in-the-ditch from the top side.

Nightweave

by Libby Lehman, 1996, Houston, Texas, 48" x 44". *Finished with a back-edge binding.*

SIGNING YOUR QUILT

I sign all my quilts in the lower right corner on the front side. You can do this with a fine-line, permanent marker if the fabric is light. On dark fabrics, I have used a metallic paint pen, but became concerned that the paint may deteriorate the fabric in time. Now I sign my name in thread using free-motion stitching. I also include the copyright sign and the year I completed the quilt.

Outback Rain

by Libby Lehman, 1996, Houston, Texas, 38" x 40". Collection of Deborrah Henry. *Hand-dyed silk ribbon and circles of organza were added before the appliqués' raw edges were satin stitched.*

LABELING YOUR QUILT

Labels are an important step in documenting and protecting your quilt. Katie Pasquini Masopust recovered a lost quilt only because she had attached a label with her name, city, and state! My labels include the name of the quilt, its size, the copyright sign, my name, complete address, and telephone number. I include the size so that I don't have to measure or look it up every time I send a quilt to a show. It also lets prospective buyers know whether it will fit their space. You might want to include other notes, such as care instructions or history about the quilt.

There are many different ways to make a label. I am a calligrapher, so my labels are handwritten. I mark guidelines on freezer paper with a permanent marker and iron it onto the back of the fabric. Always allow extra fabric on all sides. I write all the information on the fabric using a light table, then peel off the paper. Trim the excess fabric, leaving at least a ½" margin all around. Press the margins to the back. Hand stitch the completed label in the lower right corner of the quilt back.

My Quilt
20"×25"L
© Jane Quilter 1997
123 Main Street
Anytown, TX 00123
555-012-3456

MAKING A SLEEVE

If you plan to hang your quilt, a sleeve or fabric tube is the best option. A sleeve helps a quilt to hang straight and evenly distributes its weight. I make the sleeve from the same fabric as the quilt back. If you must piece a sleeve, use flat-fell seams or line it. Rods invariably get caught on the seams and can tear the sleeve. I do not sew the sleeve in with the binding because the sleeve gets more wear and tear than any other part of the quilt. If the sleeve needs replacing, I don't want to have to restitch the binding.

Utilitarian Sleeve

A simple sleeve is the answer for small quilts (less than 20" x 20") or quilts that are not going to be exhibited.

1. Cut a length of fabric the width of the quilt and 6" wide. Fold the ends under ¼", then under ¼" again, and stitch.

Wrong side

2. Fold the sleeve in half lengthwise, wrong sides together, and stitch along the length using a ¼"-wide seam allowance. Press the seam to one side. Place the sleeve, seam side down, next to the binding along the top of your quilt. Iron in place with ¼"-wide strips of fusible web along both the top and bottom. Hand stitch in place.

Seam on back side of sleeve

Exhibition Sleeve

Make an exhibition sleeve for any quilt larger than 20" x 20". This type of sleeve helps to eliminate the roll that sometimes appears when quilts are hung on a pipe (the usual hanging system at quilt shows).

1. Begin by cutting a sleeve 9" wide by the width of your quilt. Fold the 9" ends under twice and stitch close to the fold (see the illustration below step 1 on page 93). Your sleeve will now be about an inch narrower than your quilt.

2. Fold the sleeve in half lengthwise, wrong sides together, and press. This temporary pressed line is only a guide.

Press fold for guide. Right side

3. Open the sleeve and fold the edges to the middle pressed line, wrong sides together. Steam press these new fold lines firmly. These will be your hand-sewing lines.

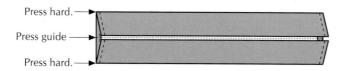

Press hard. Press guide Press hard.

4. With wrong sides and raw edges together, stitch along the length of the sleeve using a ¼"-wide seam allowance. Begin this seam about ½" from the end, backstitch to the edge, then continue stitching to the other end and backstitch again. Backstitching prevents the thread tails from hanging out the ends of the sleeve.

5. Press this center seam to one side, being careful not to press over the hand-sewing lines. The side without the seam will be convex.

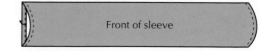

Front of sleeve

6. Place the sleeve, seam side down, ½" from the top edge of the quilt. The sleeve will be about ½" shorter on each end than the quilt. Press in place with ¼"-wide strips of fusible web along both the top and bottom. Hand stitch, being careful not to stitch through to the quilt front. Take a few reinforcing stitches in each corner.

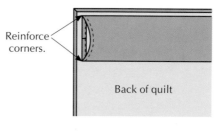

Reinforce corners.

Back of quilt

TIP

For quilts wider than 50", make two sleeves and leave a space between them. This space allows room for a vertical support in the center of the quilt, to help distribute the weight.

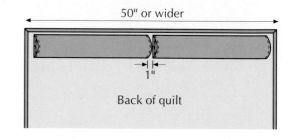

50" or wider

1"

Back of quilt

You can hang a quilt from any kind of rod. I prefer to use 2" wood strips cut to the width of the quilt. Paint the strips the same color as the quilt back or the wall. Drill a small hole near the top edge of each end. You can nail through the hole or string fishing line to hang.

BLOCKING A QUILT

Sometimes, despite your best efforts, a quilt will not hang straight. Don't despair—you can still save it. I block my quilts in the same way you block a sweater or needlepoint. I do this on my work wall, but friends have done it on Sheetrock. Please do a test run before you try it on your den wall, since there are too many variables to guarantee it won't damage the wall.

1. Pin a piece of string across the wall. Make sure it is level by measuring down from the ceiling. Use rustproof straight pins to pin the quilt to the wall. You can pin into Sheetrock by holding the pin with a pair of pliers. Pin at close intervals so that the top is horizontal and even with the string. I like to pin just inside the binding. This keeps the edge straight.

2. Drop a plumb line down one side of the quilt at the farthest point. A plumb bob can be purchased at a hardware store, or you can tie any heavy object to a sturdy string. This gives you a true vertical line. Pull the quilt out to the line and pin in place. Pin as often as needed. Repeat on the other side.

3. Measure up from the floor and pin the bottom edge until it is even horizontally.

4. Wet a press cloth or piece of washed muslin. Pin the wet press cloth over a section of the quilt. With your iron set on wool or cotton, iron the press cloth until it is dry. The three layers of the quilt absorb the moisture; the top will be damp but not dripping wet. Repeat the process until the entire quilt is damp. Leave the quilt on the wall for awhile to set it. I live in a humid climate, so I leave it up at least a day. When the quilt is set, remove the pins and gloat!

If you don't have a work wall and your quilt is not too far out of shape, try pinning it square to your carpet. Spray with warm water and let it dry. You can press with an iron, but be careful. Nylon carpeting can melt in a flash if you touch it with a hot iron.

Blocking a quilt with a wet press cloth

TIP

While I have blocked my quilts for years without any problem, I do have some words of caution. I always prewash my fabrics and use top-quality threads and batting (both cotton and polyester). If you are unsure of the colorfastness or durability of any part of your quilt, please test first.

About the Author

Libby Lehman is an internationally renowned maker of art quilts whose work is in many private, corporate, and museum collections. She has taught extensively in the United States as well as in Australia, New Zealand, Japan, Germany, and Switzerland. She and her husband, Lester, live in Houston, Texas. They have a son, Les, Jr., who is an acclaimed fly fisherman.

Resource List

Many fine shops and vendors are not listed. Be sure to check out local sources.

Artfabrik
847-931-7684
FAX 847/931-7684
www.artfabrik.com
Hand-dyed threads and fabrics

Benartex, Inc.
212/840-3250
FAX 212/921-8204
www.benartex.com
Fabrics

Bernina of America
630/978-2500
FAX 630/978-8215
www.berninausa.com
Sewing machines and accessories

CCE Supplies and Digitizing
763/862-8423
FAX 763-757-1867
www.ccesd.com
Stabilizers and embroidery supplies

Free Spirit Fabrics
212/279-0888
FAX 212/279-9382
www.freespiritfabric.com
Fabrics

JT Trading Corp
203/270/7744
FAX 203/752-8746
www.sprayandfix.com
Spray adhesives

Brewer Quilting & Sewing Supplies, Inc.
800-676-6543
FAX 630-978-9784
www.brewersewing.com
All types of quilting supplies, including OESD product

Roxanne Products Company
209/983-8700
FAX 209/983-8253
www.thatperfectstitch.com
Glue-Baste-It and notions

Superior Threads
435/652-1867
FAX 435/628-6385
www.superiorthreads.com
Threads and notions

Web of Thread
800/955-8185
FAX 425/481-0875
www.webofthread.com
Threads and notions